Venture Capital

A Practical Guide to
Fund Formation and Management

Other Books by Hambleton Lord
and Christopher Mirabile

Fundamentals of Angel Investing
A Guide to the Principles, Skills and Concepts
Every Investor Needs to Succeed

Angel Investing by the Numbers
Valuation, Capitalization, Portfolio Construction and
Startup Economics

Leaders Wanted: Making Startup Deals Happen
Advanced Techniques in Deal Leadership and
Due Diligence for Early Stage Investors

Guide, Advise, Inspire
How Startup Boards Drive Growth and Exits

Venture Capital

A Practical Guide to
Fund Formation and Management

Hambleton Lord
Christopher Mirabile

Seraf
Compass
Publications

www.seraf-investor.com

Table of Contents

Appendix

Preface

Whether traveling for business or pleasure, I enjoy visiting ancient historic sites around the world. During a recent trip, I had the occasion to visit Byblos in Lebanon. This ancient city was first settled as far back as 8800 BC, and is considered the oldest continuously inhabited city in the world. Built as the first city of the ancient Phoenicians, Byblos thrived through many millennia under the rule of the Phoenicians, Egyptians, Greeks and Romans, and was a wealthy city known for shipbuilding and trading. Entrepreneurship was alive and thriving in Byblos over five thousand years ago!

Today, Byblos is best known for its ancient ruins and it is the tourist trade that primarily supports the community. No longer a center for shipbuilding or trade on the Mediterranean Sea, the city now focuses on hosting visitors from around the world via a largely hospitality and service-based economy. So, you can imagine my surprise when I stumbled upon a sign for Neopreneur, a local co-working space that provides mentorship, workshops and meetups for entrepreneurs. What dramatic changes to our cultural landscape are we witnessing when the tourist economy in an ancient city like Byblos features a community to support entrepreneurship?

Travel to almost any part of the world these days and you are likely to run into clusters of entrepreneurship just like you will find at Neopreneur. Whether you are located in a hotbed of technology like Silicon Valley, a huge emerging market such as China, or in the ancient city of Byblos, chances are you will stumble upon a collection of entrepreneurs working to create new, vibrant companies. And, wherever you find entrepreneurs, you will find investors looking to finance those entrepreneurs.

The majority of entrepreneurs must bootstrap their businesses to success (i.e. fund them with a combination of personal resources and revenue/credit from the business). However, a meaningful percentage of high-growth-potential startups are financed by outside capital provided by investors. Historically, much of that capital came from individual angel investors or from venture capital firms. These sources of capital were specialized in making investments in fast growing technology and life science companies because of the potential for large investment returns. And historically, most of the companies, and their investors, were relatively concentrated in a handful of locations in the US and other developed countries.

But much has changed over the last few decades. There's been an explosion of entrepreneurship in many parts of the world. Major US centers like Silicon Valley, Boston and New York still hold the title for most dollars invested (and returned), but smaller cities all over the globe are becoming hotbeds of entrepreneurship with their own local sources of investment capital.

When Christopher and I began investing in early stage companies almost two decades ago, entrepreneurs trying to build high-growth investor-financed companies had a limited number of places to go for equity capital. Most assumed they would need to pitch venture capitalists, though a few knew or discovered that they could get their seed funding from angels. Today, in addition to traditional tech VCs and angel investors, there are a wide variety of capital sources for startup entrepreneurs to tap into.

New Sources of Equity Capital for Early Stage Companies

- **Social Impact Funds** - Provide capital to companies or organizations with the purpose of generating measurable returns for social outcomes alongside financial returns.

- **University Funds** - Provide capital to companies that were founded by members of the university community (e.g. professors, students, alumni). In some, but not all cases, the technology was developed while the founders worked at the university.

- **Corporate Funds** - Provide capital to companies that are developing products or technologies that have a strategic fit with the corporation's current or future plans.

- **Accelerator Funds** - Provide mentoring, co-working space, workshops, and potentially investment capital to help accelerate the growth of very early stage companies.

- **Seed Funds** - Provide capital to very early stage companies. The funds are frequently started by active angel investors as a way to invest more capital into more companies than the investor would be able to do with their own capital.

- **Country/State/Regional Funds** - Provide capital using government funds as an investment into companies that will benefit the local economy through ways such as job creation.

This book is written for fund managers who are creating these new sources of entrepreneur-focused capital today, and those who aspire to start funds in the near future. As active early stage investors, Christopher and I understand many of the challenges faced by fund managers no matter what type of fund they are running. In addition to our personal angel investing, we are experienced managers of several seed funds. And, over the years we worked with fund managers and syndicated dozens of deals with each of the other types of funds listed above.

Experience has taught us there is more to running a successful venture fund than finding companies and hoping for big exits. In the following chapters, we will discuss:

7 Critical Questions That All Venture Fund Managers Need To Consider

- What are the key factors to consider in defining your fund's investment strategy?

- How do you go about raising capital for your fund?

- What are some of the biggest challenges faced by a fund manager?

- How do you structure a fund from both a legal and accounting standpoint?

- What types of skills do you need on your fund's management team?

- What are the economics behind running a fund?

- How should a fund manager report fund activity and results to the fund stakeholders (i.e. investors or Limited Partners)?

Running an early stage venture fund can be interesting and rewarding work. But setting up and managing an investment fund takes significant time and effort. Given the relatively long life cycle of a startup company investment -- typically 10+ years before a successful investor outcome -- fund managers must be willing to commit their time and effort for at least a decade. Not everyone is willing to commit at that level. Whether you are thinking about setting up a new fund or already managing an active fund, make sure you know what the best practices are in fund management. This book will help you grasp the magnitude of the effort and determine whether you have what it takes to be successful.

Chapter 1

Charting a Course: Building a Winning VC Fund Strategy

Growing up in rural New England followed by 4 years as an English Major in college, I was always drawn to the writings of Henry David Thoreau. Fortunate to enjoy the luxury of spending much of his life as a naturalist, essayist and philosopher, Thoreau made some very keen observations that can apply to many aspects of our modern world. You might think there is no connection between Thoreau and managing a venture fund, yet one of my favorite quotes by Thoreau provides an ideal foundation for this chapter.

"It's not enough to be busy, so are the ants. The question is, what are we busy about?"

As a newly minted manager of a venture fund, your initial response to the question "what are we busy about?" might be, "finding great companies, investing in them and waiting for big financial returns." And, while your response would be directionally correct, it would be woefully incomplete. There is so much more to running a fund than leaping in, chasing companies and slinging cash around. Putting in place a well-thought-out investment strategy is a crucial component when building a high- performing portfolio of early stage companies, especially if that portfolio is going to generate acceptable returns.

Many investors think having the connections, foresight and skill to invest in big winners such as Facebook, Amazon or Google are the key factors in the success of an early stage fund. And, yes, any fund would be successful if it ended up invested in one of those 1000x return deals. But, in reality, that type of successful investment is extremely rare. No fund manager should set out to build their portfolio by assuming they will invest in one of these deals as the core part of their investment strategy. That is like setting out to win a golf tournament by getting holes in one. Instead, they should pace themselves while they work their way through the course shot by shot.

Ham's career in the startup world began in the early 1980s launching three successful software companies. He transitioned to investing in startups in 2000. So over the past four decades he was funded by or co-invested with and sat on company boards with dozens of venture funds and hundreds of venture capitalists. Through managing his personal investments and working with and discussing the investment business with VCs all over the world, he developed an understanding of how many VCs go about building their fund's investment strategy. Let's take a look at the key insights he learned over many decades of experience with funds.

Q

Ham, when you meet with a VC what are some of the first questions you ask to determine what their core investment strategy is?

When I sit down for the first time with a VC, I get right to the heart of the discussion with the sort of 20 "person/place/thing" questions that will allow me to broadly categorize the fund. In figuring out their core investment strategy, I start off by asking the following questions.

- **Industry** - What industries will you focus on? Does your fund go after a wide range of companies, or do you have certain areas of expertise where you focus? It's not unusual for a fund to have an investment thesis where they invest in one or more core technologies such as artificial intelligence, blockchain or consumer-focused e-commerce just to pick a couple examples. Or a fund can focus on companies chasing specific types of customers or markets. And, there

are types of funds that are more opportunistic and will make investment decisions based primarily on the quality of the management team.

- **Stage** - How early do you invest in the life cycle of a company? Do you like to invest at the earliest point in time (i.e. two founders and a powerpoint presentation)? Or do you prefer a more developed business with predictable revenues, etc.? Essentially, I am trying to gauge whether the fund is a Seed stage fund, a Series A/B stage fund, or a growth/later stage fund.

- **Geography** - Where do you invest? If you specialize in a very specific niche type of company, you might have to look for investments all over the world. That means a lot of time spent traveling, both to find deals and then to sit on boards. Many VCs like to stay closer to home where they can leverage their local personal network to help portfolio companies and spend less time on airplanes.

7

- **Size** - How large is your fund? What size investments does your fund make? How many investments do you target making annually and over the life of the fund?

- **Fund Maturity** - I like to get a sense of where a fund is in its own life cycle. Funds tend to add new companies most actively during the first third of their life cycle, do follow-on investments during the second and harvest exits during the final third. Enterprises operating multiple funds at once can blur this pattern, so I like to get a sense of what kind of operation they are running and where the specific fund in question is in its life cycle.

By setting specific targets for industry, stage and geography and knowing where they are in the life cycle of their fund, most investors are able to narrow down the field of potential investments for their funds. In addition, there are other overlay criteria for company selection that I see being put in place these days. The following speciality funds further narrow their investment strategy in a variety of ways.

Social Impact Funds - By combining the ability to **generate measurable social outcomes alongside financial returns**, these funds hope to benefit specific segments of the world's population (e.g. improving healthcare or promoting education in developing nations). They don't invest like traditional VCs and their limited partners (i.e. investors) tend to value social responsibility above financial returns. My questions for a social impact investors tend to focus on:

- What causes are most important to their fund?

- What level of financial return is acceptable to them?

- How do they measure impact?

University Funds - Taking advantage of the incredible resources of local research has led many universities to put in place funds to **invest in the professors and students** who are looking to start new ventures **based on the research they undertook in**

university labs. The goal of these funds is twofold: 1) to generate successful outcomes that burnish the reputation of the institution and its people, and 2) to generate financial returns that can support the long term university budget. In addition, many alumni groups are launching funds to invest in companies that are closely tied to their alma mater based on one or more alumni co-founders. My questions for university investors tend to focus on:

- What resources from your alumni network can you apply to an investment?

- What are the terms of the university's ownership in the company? (e.g. do you have equity, will there be royalty payments, etc.)

Corporate Funds - With the ever-increasing pace of technology development, and the broader trend of larger companies "outsourcing" some of their R&D to startups, large corporations struggle to stay up-to-date with rapidly changing markets. Given the slow and cumbersome nature of internal development projects, these corporations are looking to work more closely with startups around the world who may be more nimble and fast-moving innovators. Corporate venture funds are one way for these organizations to **connect with companies that have a strategic fit with the corporation's current or future plans**. My questions for corporate investors tend to focus on:

- In which areas related to your industry are you most interested in making an investment?

- When you invest, is it with the intention of acquiring the company at some future date?

- Is there a services component to your investing agreement?

Country/State/Regional Funds - Ensuring that the local population has access to well-paid employment opportunities in emerging industries is a role that many governments (both local and national) are engaged in today. These funds tend to **value job creation above financial returns**, but ultimately, a gainfully employed

9

population will generate significant local tax to help fill government coffers. My questions for government investors tend to focus on:

- What industries do you see becoming most important for future job creation in your region?

- Besides job creation, what factors help influence your investment decision? (e.g. investment returns, community development)

- What future restrictions, if any, do you place on the companies in which you invest? (e.g. headquarters location, job creation targets, etc.)

As a fund manager, if you are able to outline your industry, stage and geographic focus, apply any specific additional criteria (e.g. social impact) and understand the implications of size and fund maturity, you are well on your way to establishing your core investment strategy. Knowing what types of companies you will focus on is the cornerstone of your strategy. When you announce to the world that you are looking to make investments in early stage companies, you will be inundated with potential opportunities. Trust me... I get emails every day of the year from aspiring entrepreneurs all over the world! 99% of them don't fit my investment criteria. Putting in place a screening criteria that allows you to give a decisive "No" quickly and efficiently is a critical time saver for you and the companies who approach you.

> Knowing what types of companies you will focus on is the cornerstone of your strategy.

Q

When you invest capital out of your fund, what percent of the fund should you typically allocate for each company you invest in?

No matter what the size of your venture fund, it's important to establish several parameters to guide your **capital allocation strategy**. It's not as simple as saying, "We expect to make 20 investments from this fund and will allocate 5% of the fund to each company we invest in." Fund managers need to think about how they want to stage capital into companies. There are certainly "one and done" funds which only put one check into a company. However, most fund managers build their fund using a process which balances early valuations against later knowledge. Specifically, they do this by putting a comparatively smaller initial amount into a company and then increasing their position in later rounds (sometimes significantly) as they gain knowledge about how a company is performing.

Fund managers who are driven by financial returns as a primary measure of success will think about capital allocation along the following lines:

- How many companies do we expect to put into the fund (i.e. our minimum acceptable diversification)?

- What is the expected size of our first investment into each company?

- How much capital do we plan on reserving for follow-on rounds?

- What is our target maximum fund allocation per company?

So let's see if we can help you answer each of these questions for your particular fund. To help guide this exercise, we will base our discussion on the following example.

We just raised a $75M fund and there are three General Partners (GPs) who are managing the fund. Furthermore, we are active investors and expect to take either a board seat or a board observer seat with each company in our portfolio.

To answer the first question -- "How many companies do we expect to put into the fund?" we have to determine how many companies each of the three GPs can actively manage with close attention, advice, introductions and typically a board seat. Remember, a board

11

seat is a significant time commitment, and will limit how many investments any one individual can make. A rough estimate results in each GP being able to make and supervise a maximum of 3 to 6 investments from the fund, resulting in a portfolio of at least 9 and as many as 18 investments. If you don't need to have board oversight on every investment, the investment count can climb a bit, as long as you are able to stay on top of your overall portfolio.

> Remember, a board seat is a significant time commitment, and will limit how many investments any one individual can make.

To keep the math easy, let's say we make 15 investments from the portfolio. For the sake of simplicity, we are going to ignore the fact that our $75M fund has to pay management fees to the GPs. We are going to deem the full $75M is available to invest. In this case, if we hypothetically divide the money evenly, we could allocate $5M for each of the 15 companies in our portfolio. That's a good starting point to help us determine how large our first check could be for each company. Please note that we said "first check." It's our strong conviction, and the conviction of most of the experienced investors we have worked with, that successful early stage investors always reserve capital for follow-on rounds of investment.

Why do investors take this phased approach instead of jumping right in when the valuation is at its lowest and they can get the biggest stake? Because they are balancing the trade off between good valuation and better information.

Early seed rounds are very hard to price. The company isn't worth much because they are still early in their product development and usually have minimal revenue. So investors and entrepreneurs come up with a valuation that works for both, but that valuation is usually well above what the company is truly worth - as Christopher likes to joke: how much should you pay for two engineers, a powerpoint and a dog? As the company matures and raises additional rounds, valuations tend to approach reality. So these rounds are actually a better deal since the risk/reward ratio improves for the investor. And, because more time has passed, you are closer to exit, so even if your return multiple is lower due to the higher valuation, your IRR is higher because the money was not tied up as long.

> Why do investors take this phased approach instead of jumping right in when the valuation is at its lowest and they can get the biggest stake? Because they are balancing the trade off between good valuation and better information.

Back to allocating capital, the size of the first check is driven by a variety of factors, including:

- Quality of the deal terms (including valuation)

- The risk/return profile at the company's current stage

- Strength of the founding team

Although we vary our check size by quite a bit, as a general rule of thumb, Christopher and I put approximately 30% of our overall expected investment into the first round of financing that we participate in. In our experience, this percentage allocation is a reasonably typical thing to do. Continuing with our example, that would result in a $1.5M check for the initial round. We aim to have this size check result in a significant ownership percentage in each early stage company. If you ask experienced VCs, they will tell you they like to target a 15-25% ultimate ownership range in each of their portfolio companies. They look to hit this percentage during the first round, and then maintain this percentage by exercising their Pro-Rata Rights in future financing rounds.

This first check size (representing 30% of the allocation earmarked for potential investment in this company) gets us a meaningful amount of money put to work and takes advantage of the early valuation. It does not put too much money "blindly" at risk when there

13

are still a ton of questions unanswered. As we discuss below, if things go well, we continue to invest the other 70% over time. If things go badly, we have only about a third of the exposure we might have if we had jumped in with both feet at the start.

So for those of you still following along with this exercise, we have just invested $1.5M into the first round of 15 companies for a total of $22.5M. That leaves us with $52.5M of the $75M fund to invest in future rounds. Do we allocate all the remaining capital equally across the portfolio, or do we invest more capital into a few companies at the expense of the others?

We invest more heavily in some than others, and here's why. **With your first investment, what you are really buying on one level is an informational advantage**. You have a front row seat to see how the company does. As the losers become obvious, you will fight the urge to throw good money after bad. As the winners become apparent, you begin following on with "smarter" money as your knowledge and conviction builds,

leading to larger holdings and a higher portfolio concentration for those winning investments.

Ultimately, our portfolio of companies might end up with one group of companies receiving $1.5M+/-. In another group, we invest at a level close to our $5M per company target. And, in a small group of our high performers, we might invest as much as $10M. Betting big on your winners and allocating less on your losers is a capital allocation strategy designed to create a winning portfolio. We know picking the winners is easier said than done (especially when they come back looking for more money before their fate is fully assured), but with patience and a thoughtful approach it is doable much of the time. And as you are going along, you might want to make adjustments, for example, due to changing market conditions. Best practices dictate that you should always review your allocation strategy as you're deciding whether to invest in a new round of financing.

Q

Can you explain the life cycle of a venture fund and how it affects the timing of your investments?

Most venture funds have a 10 year time horizon to invest all of their capital and then return the profits to the fund's investors. There are exceptions to this 10 year life cycle, but that is fairly standard. Many 10 year funds end up being extended an additional 2-3 years, by consent, to clean up and distribute out the final portfolio holdings. There are also so-called "evergreen" funds, which behave in a different way from traditional funds, but we will discuss them in a bit.

> During this initial investment period, phase one of the fund, your primary focus is to discover new companies, invest in the best opportunities, and build a great portfolio of companies.

So, we are looking at a 10+ year horizon for our hypothetical fund. If that seems long, keep in mind that investing in early stage companies is rarely a quick path to riches. Your returns only come at the end when someone pays to buy your shares in the company (either an acquirer of the company, a later investor, or an over-the-counter investor in the company after an IPO.) Given that time period, understanding what it takes to have a successful exit with companies in your portfolio is a critical skill that all VCs need to develop. Although the occasional early exit can happen within one or two years of your initial investment, most companies take at least five years, and often eight or more years, to both reach a scale that will attract buyers and a transaction that can provide significant returns to the investors. Returning to the question about timing of investments, and keeping the long time horizon in mind, it should come as no surprise that most venture funds look to build their baseline portfolio of companies within the first 1.5 to 3 years of launching the fund.

That means, continuing with the example of our $75M fund from the previous question, the fund will need to invest in 15 companies in about 3 years. During this initial investment period, phase one of the fund, your primary focus is to discover new companies, invest in the best opportunities, and build a great portfolio of companies. You should add 5 to 7 new fund investments to the portfolio each year. After phase one, you should be careful about adding any new investments in very early stage opportunities. Because from about year four onward, there isn't enough time in a 10 year fund to get those early companies all the way through to an exit. You will be stuck with illiquid and hard-to-transfer holdings when you are trying to wrap the fund up.

Phase two of the fund is the period when investors help their portfolio companies grow by continuing to provide guidance and support, and by investing additional capital through follow-on rounds of financing. During this phase, some of your companies will stumble and a few might even fail. That's to be expected. However, if you've done your job right and selected some

solid companies with good management teams, parts of your portfolio will show signs of real progress. During this phase, you should deploy most of the fund's remaining capital. You should hold a little back for emergency portfolio company top-ups and fund expenses, but not too much - any money you hold back is money you cannot use to generate a return for your fund's LPs. This deployment of remaining capital occurs during years 2 through 5. You might also have a few positive exits during this phase, but you typically wouldn't expect to be in a position to return much capital to your investors with these earlier exits.

Phase two of the fund is the period when investors help their portfolio companies grow by continuing to provide guidance and support, and by investing additional capital through follow-on rounds of financing.

The final phase of a fund's life cycle is all about harvesting your returns. Phase three is a time when investors work closely with portfolio company management teams to drive towards an exit. Exits don't just happen. They require constant supervision from the company board and alignment with the management team.

> The final phase of a fund's life cycle is all about harvesting your returns. Phase three is a time when investors work closely with portfolio company management teams to drive towards an exit.

A quick final note on those evergreen funds we briefly mentioned above. These funds have investors who put in an initial amount of capital into the fund and are happy to let any returns from the fund be recycled and reinvested into new companies. This structure is very common in funds set up by government organizations (such as economic development agencies) or other types of non-profit groups who do not need a direct financial return, but rather are looking for indirect returns such as new jobs created, alumni and professors supported, or life-saving technology developed. These evergreen funds have very different life cycles and are driven less by the fund's GPs and more by original investors.

As you can see, there is an almost infinite number of ways to go about designing a fund, and many of the issues are quite complex. Decisions taken early on in the process can have significant and long-lasting effects. New fund managers are wise to seek out resources like this book as well as the advice of experienced fund managers and LPs to ensure they are putting together a fund concept that will stand the test of time and deliver the expected results. This is a very quantified and transparent industry. A little extra thought and planning is worth the effort because if you succeed, you will be rewarded handsomely, but if you fail, you are pretty much done with this kind of work as a career option.

17

Chapter 2

Venture Capital Prospecting: How To Raise a VC Fund

Staying on top of the early stage investing world requires a lot of reading. In the course of a single day, Christopher and I scan dozens of articles, newsletters, blog posts, and the occasional book chapter or industry podcast. We also read three or four newsletters which focus on activities within the venture community.

One of the biggest trends we witnessed over the past few years is the rapid pace of new early stage venture fund formation combined with significant growth in the amount of capital invested.

A decade or two ago, most of the new funds were traditional VC funds located in technology hubs in the US and a few other countries around the globe. These days, funds are popping up almost everywhere. Growth in venture investing has more than doubled in the US over the past decade as shown in the chart below. If you add statistics from the rest of the world to this data, the growth is even more dramatic.

In addition to traditional VC funds, there is significant growth from new types of investors focused on Corporate, Government, University and Social Impact goals. Corporate investors, in particular, are having a major impact on the investment community. As you can see in the two charts on the next page, in just under 10 years, US Corporate Venture has gone from ~25% of total venture investment dollars to ~44% of the total dollars.

- Some attribute this to a trend to reduce capital risk by "outsourcing" research and development to startups who are financed by third parties and then investing in or acquiring the ones showing promise.

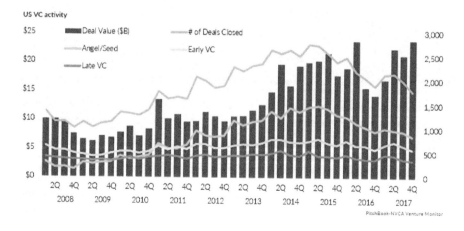

US VC activity

PitchBook-NVCA Venture Monitor

- Others attribute this to a desire to allow more innovation to flourish indirectly despite the more mature conservative corporate culture by owning minority investments in nimble start ups.

- And still others attribute it to a desire to have an inside track on acquiring attractive start-ups before they raise a ton of venture capital and have their required acquisition price go through the roof.

Regardless of why it is happening, it is clearly an important trend in our current market.

A decade or two ago, most of the new funds were traditional VC funds located in technology hubs in the US and a few other countries around the globe. These days, funds are popping up almost everywhere.

US corporate VC participation activity

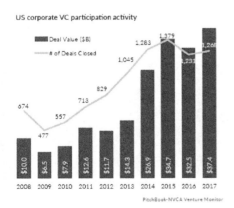

PitchBook-NVCA Venture Monitor

US corporate VC participation % of total VC

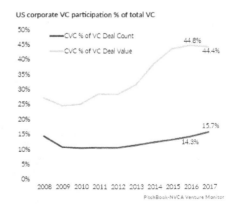

PitchBook-NVCA Venture Monitor

In addition, angel investing is reaching new heights in terms of deals and investment dollars. Angel investments are coming from multiple sources, including groups of angels working together in networks both formal and informal, networks of angels coming together into syndicates, angel funds, family offices, and syndication platforms (such as AngelList, etc.). Just in the past 8 years, total US-based angel investments per year have grown close to 4X. And the numbers shown in the chart below represent just the data that Pitchbook was able to gather. We have seen data from other sources that support activity levels more than twice that shown in this chart.

So what does all this mean? Why should you care? Well, if you are interested in raising a new fund, there appears to be a lot of capital available to invest into early stage companies. And as even better news, this is a very difficult and time-intensive asset class. Most sources of significant capital don't have the time or the inclination to be an active investor in this sector. Direct investment in smaller deals in early companies are so much work compared to other kinds of investment opportunities available to them. And the failure rate is high, so diversification into a relatively large number of deals is essential. However, for reasons of asset allocation and the desire to chase

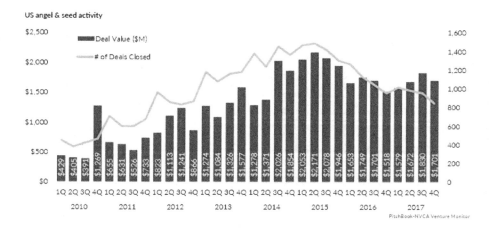

US angel & seed activity

higher returns, those with significant assets to invest are highly motivated to find a way to participate in the tremendous upside potential offered by this asset class. So committing their money to an early stage venture fund actively managed by experts becomes an attractive option to them (at least in theory).

But how do you go about convincing these prospective investors to trust you with their hard earned capital? Christopher is both a Limited Partner in several venture funds and a General Partner in a couple of seed funds. He has sat on both sides of the fund raising table. He understands what it's like to be asked to invest in a fund and knows what questions he likes to ask the fund manager. And, he understands what it takes to raise capital from outside investors for the funds he manages. Let's hear what advice he has to offer to a first time fund manager looking to raise a new venture fund.

Q

Christopher, before we dig into issues around fundraising, can you explain the roles played by a venture fund's General Partners (GPs) and the fund's Limited Partners (LPs)?

The General Partners (GPs) of a fund are a team of experienced investors and/or operators who actively run the day-to-day management of the fund, invest its capital, and manage the portfolio. A General Partner (GP) may serve on the board of one or several portfolio companies ensuring the fund's stake in the investment is looked after.

A Limited Partner (LP) is a qualified investor who commits a certain amount of capital to a fund and pays a management fee (or carry) to the GP to manage his/her investment. LPs may be experienced investors themselves or entirely new to investing. Depending on the fund arrangement, some LPs may be passive investors who solely provide capital, while other LPs may actively participate in a fund by sourcing deals, serving as an industry expert, conducting due diligence, or providing connections or other resources that could help with analyzing the opportunity, enabling growth or identifying exit opportunities.

The terms "limited partner" and "general partner" date back to the early years of venture capital before limited liability companies (LLCs) existed when nearly all the funds in the nascent industry were structured as somewhat complex partnerships with LPs and GPs entering into a partnership agreement spelling out how work would be divided, fees would be assessed and profits would be distributed.

These agreements were complex and carefully designed to minimize legal liability and maximize tax efficiency. Today's funds are very similar in concept, but can be structured quite differently using limited liability companies (LLCs) and limited liability partnerships (LLPs). Or, a modern fund can even be structured as a combination of LLCs and a traditional partnership

agreement whereby the GP is an LLC entity rather than a person or group of people. The fee and profit sharing arrangements in modern funds can be far more complex. As the industry has matured, GPs and LPs have both become more clever, but the goals and the roles remain the same: active investors manage money on behalf of passive partners while minimizing liability and maximizing tax efficiency.

Q

Tell us about your decision-making process before you invest in funds as a limited partner. What were some of the key questions you ask the fund managers?

Let me answer that two ways because I am a somewhat special case. First I will cover the general issues I look at, and recommend any LP review before investing. And then I will show how I applied them in my special situation.

> What kinds of performance have they delivered for past LPs?

> How consistent has that performance been over time?

> What specific companies did they invest in?

> Are they reporting performance based entirely on one single blockbuster, or have they shown an ability to identify and nurture multiple solid winners?

> What was their personal role in those investments (lead or just a bystander)?

In addition, you will want to investigate the following:

> What other professional and personal commitments do they have on their plate that might compete for their time and attention? For example, while lots of board experience is great, if they are already overloaded with board obligations, can they take on new board seats in this new portfolio?

> How connected and networked are they? How visible are they?

> In short, you are looking for a team with a track record, the skills and the time to invest this new fund successfully. It is a hard job that involves a lot of judgement and intuition. Do these GPs have the chops?

When an LP looks at a fund they should consider three different categories of questions to assess:

1. Team Capabilities

2. Fund Design

3. Fund Status and Current Investing Climate

Team Capabilities

This is really a question of looking at the GPs and figuring out whether they are a team you believe can deliver the superior performance you expect. So you are going to be looking at their general experience base in industry prior to becoming a fund manager, as well as their level of experience and past performance as a GP.

Do they have access to the best founding teams (i.e. good deal flow)?

- How good is their reputation in the community? What kinds of references can they provide from other LPs, founders, VCs?

- How diverse is the GP team? Do they bring different perspectives and complementary skills to the table?

In short, you are looking for a team with a track record, the skills and the time to invest this new fund successfully. It is a hard job that involves a lot of judgement and intuition. Do these GPs have the chops?

Fund Design

The concept of fund design really encompasses everything from the fund structure to the fund philosophy.

- What is the fee structure and carry (profit sharing percentage) and how does that compare to market norms?

- What is the size of the fund?

- What percentage of the fund is being personally invested by the GPs so they have some skin in the game alongside LPs?

- How many companies and how much diversification is the fund aiming for?

- What is the fund's strategy for initial investment vs. total investment over time (and target percentage ownership of each company)?

- Will the GPs make all the investments directly, or do they plan to employ "scouts" or other agents to represent them in some deals?

Furthermore, you will look to answer the following:

- In what stage of company will the fund invest (pre-seed, seed, angel, angel extension, pre-Series A, Series A, Series A extension, Series B, or later growth stages)?

- What is the fund's overall investment thesis - does it intend to target a particular industry,

26

sector, technology, market space, or other "theme"?

- What are the criteria the GPs plan to use when evaluating companies?

- Are there deal structures or deal terms that they will seek out or terms which they will not accept?

- What is the GPs' plan for reporting to LPs?

- What performance benchmarks do the GPs consider relevant for the fund and what is the team's expectation in terms of overall performance they will be able to deliver?

By asking these questions, you are going to get an overall sense of what this fund is trying to do that is different from other funds and how and why they believe their unique approach will lead to superior returns.

Fund Status and Fund Climate

Your final set of questions should be about establishing the broader context in which this fund raising is occurring.

- Is this the GPs' first (or tenth) fund?

- How many prior funds are still actively investing (and requiring a lot of time) and how many are in harvest mode?

- What is the GPs' current commitment level to those older funds?

- How long has this particular fund been raising money?

- How much of this fund has actually been raised so far?

- When does the fund expect to have a first close and start investing?

- Are there company investments already earmarked to be added to the fund at inception?

- Are there special terms being offered to early "anchor" LPs who are willing to come into the first close and get the fundraising ball rolling?

- What is the fundraising climate right now and are these competitive terms given the current environment?

- Who are the other LPs committed to the fund and are any of them imposing special LP investment deal terms that are different from those you are offering me, or are any of them imposing special restrictions or constraints on the fund?

As you can see, this is a huge list of questions you need to have a handle on to understand what you are getting into as an LP, and to be able to answer if you are going to raise money as a GP. For a first time GP or LP it can be pretty daunting, but with a little experience and some familiarity with some of the short-hand, it is really not too long a list.

My Situation

Consider my situation, for example, since I am a very active investor with a lot of my own direct investments and experience in the space, and I am a GP running a couple small funds. I do not fit the profile of the typical passive LP just looking for a way to get into this asset class and put some money to work. And, I am not going to pay a lot of fees for that access. Instead, in the past I sought out three very specific things: geographical diversification, some specialized vertical expertise, and a bit more quantitative diversification (i.e. more companies) than I would be able to get managing that number of investments directly myself.

Because I am already an active investor, I am not wild about the fees and carry associated with the passive investment model, so I was looking for low cost fund opportunities. And, I was looking for funds investing in early stage companies. I have portfolio allocations for each asset class, and these fund commitments were coming out of my angel allocation.

So when I looked at funds, I was going with managers I knew, using approaches I understood, in markets I was familiar with and fund designs that fit my criteria. In one case I committed to a couple of very low cost angel funds based in California that would bring geographic and quantitative diversification which I would not otherwise be able to get. I also invested in a couple of specialized EdTech funds in Boston run by managers who were experts in this interesting (to me) field and running a nationally respected EdTech accelerator that would attract some of the best companies around.

Q

What are the elements you need to have in a pitch deck or fund prospectus to convince prospective LPs to invest in your fund?

Your fund's marketing and prospectus materials need to address all three of the main topics I've discussed above (the team's capabilities, the fund's design, and the current status of the fund) in sufficient detail to at least cover the biggest and most obvious of the questions before they are asked. And, managers should be ready with answers for all of the rest of the more detailed questions - not every LP will think to ask every question, but across all the LPs as a whole, you will be asked most of those questions.

In addition, the fund materials will need to cover legal details like the requirements of LPs, a summary of the legal and structural terms of the fund, basics like investment mechanics and deadlines, and the legally advisable boilerplate protections such as risk factors and disclaimers. Each fund document will be a little different, but there are norms, and competent legal counsel with experience in the fund formation area can provide you with models and examples from which you can start.

> Your fund's marketing and prospectus materials need to address all three of the main topics -- the team's capabilities, the fund's design, and the current status of the fund.

Once you have a great set of documents, you still need to keep in mind that your documentation falls into that old category of "necessary, but not sufficient." Fundraising is a time-consuming inefficient face-to-face process. These LPs are committing serious money to you and giving you a great deal of discretion to exercise your judgement. They are going to want to get to know you and become comfortable with you. So the face-to-face meeting is the key, and the fund materials are merely what gets left behind.

Q

When you decided to start your own fund, what qualifications did you have that were important to your prospective investors?

The primary qualification I had in the eyes of my LPs was tons of experience in the early stage investing space from many years of investing my own money in startups, evaluating companies, advising startups, serving on boards and leading Launchpad Venture Group, a large group of very capable and well-respected angels. And, I had invested in some good companies with demonstrated success delivering strong returns.

Second, was personal connections. I had a large network of well-respected people in the early stage space. In one instance, the anchor LP knew someone well who had in turn known me very well for many years. So I was a trusted "friend of a friend" rather than a stranger.

Third, I possessed other applicable professional skills and professional experience from years in industry which lent me additional credibility.

This included having spent time as a corporate and securities lawyer doing venture capital fund formation work and supporting investments in startups, as well as having spent a long time inside a public technology company, including serving as the CFO dealing with Wall Street. So I was not just an inexperienced young person walking in off the street. I was someone who had been around a little bit.

And of course I was working with an equally accomplished and experienced partner with many of the same skills and also many complementary skills, and we had a long track record of working well together.

Q

How is investing from a venture fund different from angel investing?

It is at once both remarkably similar and totally different. When you are an angel representing yourself, you can be as exact or inexact with your investments and your process as you want. If you want to make money, there are certainly some best practices available, but you can decide whether or not to follow them. If you want, you can chase your interests and indulge your passions. You can build a lopsided portfolio. You can vary your investment pace. You are under no time pressure from a fund expiration or IRR deadline. You don't have any reporting responsibilities other than to yourself, and maybe to your significant other. You can jump into things without as much diligence if you want and follow your gut when the mood strikes you.

When you are running a fund, you are investing in the exact same kinds of companies and deals. That is where the similarities end. Running a fund, you are a professional manager acting as a fiduciary to LPs based on an agreed upon set of operating constraints. It is much more constrained and structured and it is much more responsibility. You have a good chunk of money you need to put to work, and you are on a clock to get

31

that money into the very best companies you can so that those companies can begin maturing and wending their way along that slow journey to exit.

> Running a fund, you are a professional manager acting as a fiduciary to LPs based on an agreed upon set of operating constraints. It is much more constrained and structured and it is much more responsibility.

You are responsible for regular reporting and tax compliance. You are looking to build a diversified and structured and balanced portfolio. You have an obligation to do an appropriate level of diligence in every deal you do and to provide as much timely oversight into those companies as you can. You are writing checks of specific sizes and paying attention to the maximum amount you put into a company. You are using a very thoughtful process of deciding whether to follow on with later investments into those portfolio companies. And you are worrying from day one about

driving liquidity and sufficient performance in a timely manner. It is an entirely different beast.

Needless to say, being an angel investor on your own account is easier and a bit more fun! But, your upside is limited to the amount of capital you can comfortably invest on your own.

Q

What are some of the critical skills and resources needed by an early stage venture fund's General Partners?

The critical skills and resources really boil down to four categories:

1. Business experience and industry knowledge

2. People skills

3. Startup knowledge

4. Connections and reputation

Business Experience and Industry Knowledge

If you have absolutely no interest in or experience with business and know nothing about how companies work, you have probably chosen the wrong field. You do not have to be an expert in everything, but to be successful, you and your fellow GPs collectively need to know something about the industries in which you are investing (including regulatory frameworks such as the FDA approval process in the healthcare space).

You will need at least some basic accounting and finance background, knowledge of how early stage investments are structured and negotiated, and how fast-growth companies finance themselves over time. It really helps to understand the different ways companies can market themselves, the different ways they go to market, the different ways companies can approach building sales capabilities, and some fundamentals about business models, revenue models, and operating models.

And, you are going to need to have at least a rudimentary understanding of how mergers and acquisitions work if you are going to be able to help your companies drive all the way to exit through acquisition. (IPOs are rare enough and the skills are specialized enough, so I am not going to include it in the already daunting list!)

People Skills

Venture capital is really a people game. You need to be good at:

- Evaluating the people behind many prospective investments

- Coaching and advising those who are dealing with company challenges and ambiguous situations, often for the first time

- Contributing on company boards

- Convincing LPs to back you

- Convincing your investing partners to join you in taking a chance on a company you believe in, and

- Convincing sought-after entrepreneurs to work with you.

There are no two ways about it - having a high emotional intelligence and good communication skills are critical to being a successful VC.

> Having experience with how startups work and what their typical bottlenecks and common problems are can go a long way toward anticipating and avoiding issues in your portfolio companies before they derail progress or bring companies down.

Startup Knowledge

Hyper-growth oriented startups like the kind you will be investing in are very unique creatures which bear little resemblance to larger enterprises you may be familiar with and regularly read about in the Wall Street Journal. To steal a phrase from Facebook, these companies "move fast and break things." They are often going after new markets with new technologies. They have fewer processes and far fewer resources than large companies. They have less to lose and cannot afford to be as patient. They need to take more risks to out-maneuver the incumbents. Bottom line, they require special care and feeding to nurture them along and that requires special knowledge and skills. Having experience with how startups work and what their typical bottlenecks and common problems are can go a long way toward anticipating and avoiding issues in your portfolio companies before they derail progress or bring companies down.

Connections and Reputation

A portfolio can only be as good as the deal flow it receives. A VC does not have to know every single person in their city, but if they are going to see interesting companies, they need to have a good reputation for integrity, fairness, and value-add. It doesn't hurt if

34

they are likable and empathetic as well. Further, they need to be plugged into the innovation ecosystem. They need to be connected to a network of investors and entrepreneurs. They need to know the key organizations such as incubators, accelerators, business plan competitions, university and research labs, other investors, funds and networks.

The fund also needs to have representatives speaking on panels, judging business plan competitions, and offering advice and mentorship. GPs may want to have a blog or social media presence. And they need to constantly nurture that good reputation as a respectful, talented, connected, and value-added investor. The better an entrepreneurial team and idea are, the more choice they will have in picking an investor. If you want to build a portfolio of great companies, you need those companies to want to work with you.

Q

How did you determine the appropriate size for the fund you manage, and how would you advise a new GP to set their fund size?

Assuming hypothetically that you can raise as much money as you want, your maximum fund size is still going to be limited by two factors:

- How big the fund's GP team is, and

- What stage of company you are investing in.

Here is why: each GP can only manage a certain number of investments at a time and the fund can only put a stage-appropriate amount of money into each company. Very early stage companies tend to raise smaller rounds as they develop the business and figure out what is working and then may later go on to raise larger amounts of money down the road.

If you are trying to invest a very large fund (say, several hundred million dollars), and you try to put it into very early stage deals, you are going to end up with a very large number of small checks into an unmanageable number of companies. This is because there is only so much money you can squeeze into a round whose total size is $500,000 or $1,000,000. Even if you could take the entire round, you wouldn't necessarily want to. At the early stages, other investors can help add value and oversight to these companies, and you'd otherwise have far too many small investments to be solely responsibility for all of them.

Conversely, if you have a very small fund (say, a few million dollars), and you try to build a portfolio of later stage investments, you are going to have a major problem with diversification. Those later rounds are much larger and, even if you could get into them (which is questionable unless you have a stellar reputation or have been with the company since inception), the minimum check size you would want to put in to be relevant to the company and the deal would gobble up your whole fund.

So overall, you are striving for a stage-appropriate balance between fund size, deal size and portfolio size (i.e. quantity). Your goal is to build a portfolio with enough companies in it that you are sufficiently diversified, but still have a manageable number of companies per GP so that you can oversee them properly.

Q

Where are some of the sources of capital that are available to new venture funds?

The question of capital sources is a good news/bad news story. The good news is that there are many different sources of capital, and in the current climate, some of these sources are more eager than ever to hand their capital over to funds, including those run by new fund managers. The bad news is that fund-raising is an opaque, inefficient, time-consuming, uncertain and very manual, face-to-face endeavor. Worse, many of the sources are hard to categorize, hard to reach and slow to come on board.

Established fund managers can get huge chunks of money from big well-known players like pension fund managers, endowments and sovereign wealth funds. New managers don't have that option. The big players are very sophisticated, very knowledgeable about the VC business, and very focused on the funds that can deliver top quartile VC industry performance.

> So as with many things in life, reaching family offices often boils down to old-fashioned networking: do you know any people who might know any people who might have connections to one or more family office?

However, there are sources of capital which are more open to betting on newer managers - if you can find them. One large source are so-called family offices which are private wealth management offices dedicated to the needs of a single family or small group of families. These offices are increasingly open to allocating some of their investment dollars into higher risk/higher return asset classes such as early stage investing. In some cases they are adding a social impact requirement layer onto the fund selection process.

In terms of locating family offices, there are some family office associations and there are conferences which cater to them, but I would not want to overstate the potential value there. The easier it is to find a family office through one of these organizations, the more likely they are to be besieged with requests for funding and the less likely they are to respond to your request, let alone respond favorably. Family offices, especially the older, larger and more sophisticated ones, are extremely hard to find and connect with. So as with many things in life, reaching family offices often boils down to old-fashioned networking: do you know any people who might know any people who might have connections to one or more family office?

Various social impact organizations and philanthropies are also increasingly open to the idea of supplementing their giving and grant-making with social impact investing approaches. Finding and approaching these organizations is somewhat easier because they are inherently more public and impact-oriented in what they do. But that ease is more than offset by the need to have a very good match between the goals of the organization and the impact goals of your fund. In particular, you are going to need to have a set of metrics to measure your fund that will need to be deemed adequate by the organization.

Another source of capital can come from other fund managers looking to diversify their fund by having another manager with a different region, skillset or focus invest part of the fund. Be forewarned, however, that these funds will be looking for discounts on fees and carry since returns would be crushed by two overlapping sets of management fees and carry. But they are still worth targeting because they understand your business, can make decisions quickly and have potentially large amounts of money to contribute to your fund.

The final source of capital comes directly from high net-worth and ultra high net-worth individuals who are willing to put a small amount of their wealth under your management - either because they know you or because they like your approach or focus area. Some of these people may be totally passive investors focusing on other areas of their life or just other investment areas, and will look to you as a pathway to invest in the very labor intensive early stage asset class. Others may already be active angels doing some of their own angel investing, but looking for additional diversification and reach beyond the number of deals they can do themselves.

In some cases these angels can be accessed through personal contacts in your community and traditional angel networks and groups which might be based in your city. (The Angel Capital Association maintains a list of angel networks organized by geography.) Good old-fashioned networking may allow you to track down some especially high net-worth angels who might be open to allocating a little money to an interesting fund.

In other cases, angels can be accessed using newer more technology-centric methods. In recent years platforms like AngelList and some crowdfunding platforms have emerged. With them come methods of aggregating angels into deals by allowing them to follow a particular investor into deals by pledging a certain per deal amount

to a "syndicate" following that investor. This world may allow you to locate some angels, but it could also allow you to get a start as a lead investor trying to build a track record of picking companies and building a portfolio. (Note this is not necessarily an endorsement of this kind of investing. While it can be really interesting and has a lot of potential, in my view there can be some important downsides to long-distance investing by remote-control. You are paying fees to follow amateur investors you know nothing about, into companies you and maybe most of your co-investors have never met. As we have noted many times, meeting the team is a very important (most likely the most important) part of evaluating a startup. So you will want to apply a bit of caution and common sense in this space.)

Are there people you can hire to help you raise your fund?

Yes, but...you will want to select your broker with care. The world of private equity (of which VC is but one subset) is incredibly broad and diverse. As you have seen above, there are myriad different sources of capital and there is an almost infinite number of different kinds of investment opportunities. In an industry that large, there are bound to be middlemen who offer to broker introductions between money and opportunity. And many of them are undoubtedly very good and highly specialized at what they do. Of course they all charge fees which are generally a function of the amount money raised.

The reason I suggest caution is that the skill with which a broker represents you can vary and you need to make sure you get good value for your fees. You will also want to be careful because these kinds of brokers can introduce issues around investor (LP) fit for your fund and/or misplaced expectations. A broker who does not have a good collection of contacts among the right group of LPs may not be able to introduce you to LPs who will be a good fit for your fund.

The reason working with brokers can be tricky for a fund are the same as with any third party middleman situation. Sophisticated investors with pools of money tend to be patient. They know the best GPs will figure out how to find them directly and they tend to be a bit skeptical of GPs who need help with fundraising. Further, you are still going to have to do the work necessary to close the deal. So, in effect, you are really just paying for an introduction. Closing the deal with a stranger you were introduced to by a third party is going to be harder than closing the deal with someone you networked to through a warm contact. Given that you have no nexxus with the LP, it increases the risk that they are not a good fit for you either, or have some unknown attributes that make them more likely to want to hide behind a broker. There can also be situations where a third party in the chain enhances the probability of a miscommunication or a misalignment of expectations.

Some of this can be mitigated by having brokers who are very specialized and whose business model is to not introduce investors to any fund unless the broker has some of their own money in that fund. That can go a long way toward upping the quality of the representation and introductions. But you still have to weigh and decide if representation is for you. You are paying for introductions you might be able to get yourself with some good old-fashioned networking. A reasonable approach is to try to raise the fund on your own using as much networking as you can possibly muster. If that doesn't work, research brokers to see if you can find a really good one who has a solid gold reputation and puts money in alongside its clients. Even then, you will naturally want to do a lot of research on the prospective LPs introduced to you by a third party before agreeing to let them into your fund.

By now it should be clear that raising a fund is quite a bit more involved than it might first appear. It takes a professional with a certain kind of experience and temperament as well as the connections to get through the right doors. The design of the fund and strategy takes a fair bit of artistry. And the actual money raising is a long, grueling and inefficient process. However, if you can get through the fundraising gauntlet, the actual running of a fund is going to be much better by comparison - it can be pretty interesting and rewarding work!

Chapter 3

Three Places At Once: Challenges VCs Face In Managing Their Time

Venture Capital is one of those professions that is idealized by many and misunderstood by most. From a distance it seems like it should be great. You are your own boss, you set your own hours, you are not stuck behind a desk, you hang around with interesting go-getters and you sling big piles of cash around. What could be better?

Venture Capital is extensively written about by the business press, discussed in depth by entrepreneurs, and seen as an excellent career choice by MBA students at top business schools all over the world. Many VCs who write, tweet and give interviews end up attaining minor celebrity-level status along the lines of professional athletes and movie stars.

And if you strike it big with an investment in a company that has a billion dollar exit, you can be looking at a major payday that will set you up for life. With that in mind, it's not a big surprise that many entrepreneurs and finance professionals look to a career in venture capital as a way to make big bucks and live a charmed life. If only it were so easy!

So...you still think you want to run a venture fund? Maybe it's a good idea to take a look at the reality. What are you actually getting yourself into?

Let's take a close look at some of the issues and challenges you will face in building a successful venture fund. In the previous chapter, we discussed the obstacles you may encounter in raising capital for your fund. That hurdle alone will stop most individuals from getting established as VCs. You would think with new venture funds popping up everywhere, it must be pretty easy to get a fund up and running. Although we don't have any hard data we can point to, based on what we have seen in the market, it wouldn't surprise us if less than 20% of those teams who set out to raise a venture fund actually succeed in raising the fund. And the ones who fail, put in a fair amount of unpaid work and travel before they ultimately give up.

Before we jump into a series of questions on the key challenges faced by VCs, let's set some context. This discussion is centered on smaller funds. By that we mean our answers will focus on challenges faced by small venture funds that raise under $100M. At the dawn of venture capital, that was a decent sized VC fund. In today's market that is small, and this size class is where the majority of new Seed Funds, Angel Funds and Social

Impact Funds would fall. Some of the answers below will also apply to Corporate and Government Funds, but their challenges are often dictated less by the responsibility of generating large financial returns and more by the long term goals and politics of the specific company or government.

> If you are a GP in a small fund, your responsibilities are wide ranging and very time consuming.

Q

Ham, outside of the fundraising challenge, what are some of the biggest challenges a General Partner at a venture fund runs into?

When I look back on the past 20 years as an active early stage investor, the biggest challenge I face is not having enough time to cover all the bases. Even if you work hard and put in long hours, it is very easy to have something boil over somewhere. If you are a GP in a small fund, your responsibilities are wide ranging and very time consuming. They include the following (and more):

- Screening your deal flow looking for interesting companies

- Meeting with entrepreneurs to evaluate whether to invest in their company

- Performing diligence, negotiating and syndicating deals, and closing investments into new companies

- Helping your portfolio companies succeed as a board member or advisor

- Meeting with and reporting out to your Limited Partners (LPs)

- Networking, networking, networking (you have to get your name out there and keep it out there!)

- Reams and reams of communications in support of everything above; in early stage investing, you better like doing lots of email, phone calls and text messages, because they will form the backdrop to everything you

45

do, and frequently extend well outside of normal business hours.

At first glance, that list of tasks doesn't sound too daunting, until you dig into each one and learn what it really takes. Each task can take dozens of hours per week if you don't do a good job with time management. And, first time VCs who don't have experienced partners in the fund will usually struggle with balancing all that's on their plate.

Q

How do you handle the challenge of managing deal flow and meeting with lots of early stage companies?

Screening your deal flow looking for interesting companies doesn't sound too difficult. In fact, it sounds pretty exciting. Who wouldn't want to evaluate cool startup companies by sitting down for a 30-60 minute coffee with some really interesting entrepreneurs? That sounds like fun to me, and it was when I first started out investing.

Let's take a look at the math behind how much time it takes for this task. A VC with a good network receives hundreds of plans a year. Each one takes a few minutes to screen to see whether it's a fit for the fund. Out of the hundreds of plans you receive in a month, maybe 10% of the plans are worth having a meeting with the company. So, 20 meetings times 30-60 minutes per meeting adds up to 10-20 hours a month. That sounds manageable... but that's not how it really works. Scheduling the meeting, travel time to the meeting, and a variety of other factors can easily extend that 30-60 minute meeting into well over an hour of real time spent. And, don't forget the demo days you attend during the month to see a quick, concentrated set of pitches from 10 or more companies. Those demo days can easily take up half a day of your time.

> First time VCs who don't have experienced partners in the fund will usually struggle with balancing all that's on their plate.

Don't get me wrong... I still enjoy meeting new entrepreneurs and hearing their pitches. These days, in order to manage my schedule efficiently, I have to be a bit more selective in the number of meetings I take. For first time venture funds, having very well-defined criteria for choosing companies is important to limit the amount of time you waste looking at plans that don't fit your firm's investment criteria. It's not unusual for a VC to invest in only 1 out of every 100 deals that cross their desk, so an efficient process is required. And, coming up with an efficient approach to scheduling and getting to meetings will save you a ton of unproductive time. Some investors will use scheduling tools in their emails, some will try to get entrepreneurs to come to them to save travel time, some will fall back to phone calls or video calls in lieu of a portion of their meetings, some will hold "office hours" where they just set aside a block of time and bang through a bunch of sessions, and some, like my crazy partner Christopher, will resort to inviting an entrepreneur to walk or ride the subway with him in between meetings!

Q

Tell us a bit about the time commitment and issues you run into when you find a company you really like and want to make an investment in.

From an initial group of 100 qualified investment opportunities, we might become seriously interested in 3 or 4 companies. After a series of hour long meetings with the CEO and her founding team, we will start a due diligence process with the company. This is a fairly time-consuming effort that can easily take 30 or 40 hours of work to complete. And, not every due diligence effort results in an investment. About 50% of companies we take into diligence end up with an investment.

When diligence is wrapping up, we start the process of negotiating the terms of a deal with the company. Experienced early stage investors should be efficient at this process, but it takes time for new investors to learn the nuances of deal negotiation. And, to complicate matters, early stage investors

47

frequently run into situations where novice investors offer the entrepreneur deal terms that are too generous. Experienced investors know it's best to walk away from the deal if the entrepreneur is willing to have dumb money drive the deal terms.

> It's not unusual for a VC to invest in only 1 out of every 100 deals that cross their desk, so an efficient process is required. And, coming up with an efficient approach to scheduling and getting to meetings will save you a ton of unproductive time.

Assuming all goes well with due diligence, and you are able to negotiate reasonable deal terms, it's time to move onto deal syndication to fill out the round. Successful VCs have a network of co-investors that they like to work with. This allows you to share some of the effort and transaction cost needed to invest in a company and support the company's future growth. It also streamlines the process of raising enough capital to properly fund the company. Just be aware, if you are the deal lead, you can expect to spend significant time and effort in this process.

Q

After you make an investment, should the General Partners (GPs) take a board seat on every company they invest in?

If you want to be involved in helping the companies, yes. Or if you don't, someone else you know well and trust very much needs to. Investor money needs to be paired with advice and oversight if it is going to generate a return. And it is not a trivial matter - taking a board seat is a big responsibility and a major time commitment. In some ways, making the initial investment is the easy part of being a VC. The real work starts after you make the investment. Between regular board meetings, phone calls with the CEO, and a cornucopia of other tasks, an engaged board member can easily put in 100 to 200 hours of work per year, per board seat. If

48

you are sitting on 3 boards, that time really adds up!

Now, back to your original question... "should GPs take a board seat on every company they invest in?"... my answer is a qualified yes. You can't help companies in your portfolio drive towards exit unless you know what the issues are and are involved with helping them through their struggles to succeed. The exception to this rule occurs when you have a lot of faith and trust in the current board members. But even then, your LPs will have every right to expect you to have semi-regular check-ins with both the CEO and the board member with whom you are working.

> Sometimes, a fund manager will take a board observer seat instead of an actual voting corporate board seat. This allows them to stay engaged, but the time commitment is significantly less than a full board seat.

Note that in some situations, you may be in the boardroom, but not actually a corporate director. Sometimes, a fund manager will take a board observer seat instead of an actual voting corporate board seat. This allows them to stay engaged, but the time commitment is significantly less than a full board seat. You advise on the problems, but you don't own responsibility and liability for them.

How should a venture fund's General Partners handle communications and reporting with their Limited Partners?

First off, you need to **set a proper level of expectations with your investors**. And that comes down to being able to objectively answer questions related to what level of returns investors should expect and over what timeframe they should expect to receive those returns. I am not suggesting you know exactly what kinds of returns you will have or precisely how long it will take; I am telling you that you will need to be honest with your investors about that. You can share your expectations and your plans for getting there, but at the end of the day, you need to be clear that this is a risky business full of unknowns. Failure to make that crystal clear will work out very poorly for you and may be the end of your venture career.

A key thing you need to understand and explain to your investors, is that it's rare that a fund invests in a small number of huge winners in venture capital. Most funds are lucky to have one big winner in their portfolio. As a General Partner, you need to know what level of returns are produced by successful venture funds. Over the past decade, top quartile funds generated annual returns in the 15% to 27% range. And, the majority of capital is typically returned to investors in the later third of a fund's history. Make sure you don't over-promise to investors on your fund's expected returns and the timeframe for those returns. Success does not happen overnight - your investors will have to be patient.

My second piece of advice relates to communications. Your investors have entrusted a fair amount of capital to the fund. Unless you set very clear expectations to the contrary, it is reasonable for your **LPs to expect regular proactive communications from you**. So, what level and frequency of communications should you plan to deliver? Most funds produce a regular report with the following items:

- A table with a list of all portfolio companies. This table should include company name, website, industry, main product/service, cost basis of investment, and current value of investment.

- A table with a list of transactions from the latest time period. This table should include company name, type of transaction, date, and value of transaction.

- A table with a list of recent valuation changes for companies in the portfolio.

- A table with a list of exited companies and the capital returned from those exits.

50

- A series of charts and tables that report on portfolio metrics such as investments and returns by calendar year, IRR, distributed to paid-in capital (DPI), total value to paid-in capital (TVPI), etc.

- For each company in the portfolio, a brief written update on the company's status and financials.

> Make sure you don't over-promise to investors on your fund's expected returns and the timeframe for those returns. Success does not happen overnight - your investors will have to be patient.

As to frequency, we believe a quarterly report with the above items covers the key elements needed by LPs to evaluate a fund's performance. The delivery of that report is sometimes supported by a conference call to discuss the results in more detail with any interested LPs. And finally, some bigger funds, or funds that have an active network of LPs, will hold an annual meeting that includes updates by the GPs along with a chance for the LPs to meet many, if not all of the CEOs of the portfolio companies.

It's important to remember, if you want to build your reputation and raise another fund, your investors will expect open, regular and honest communications from you. Keeping your LPs well informed and making positive results in your fund goes a long way towards raising your next fund.

Q

Why is networking so important for a VC?

This question might sound obvious to most readers, but it does deserve some discussion. Great entrepreneurs have access to capital from many different sources. How you differentiate yourself and make your firm a first choice for those seeking capital will make all the difference in your fund's long term success.

You will have your work cut out for you before you become well-known in the community of entrepreneurs in which you want to invest, unless you are already a well- known individual (or team) before you start your fund. It can take years to build your reputation and get access to top deals. Great deal flow is one of the greatest assets a venture fund has. One of the best ways to build your reputation and get access to great deal flow is to be seen on a regular basis in your community. So how do you go about doing that? Here is a short list of a few approaches we have seen work in our community:

- Attend events where your target entrepreneurs spend time

- Sit on panels where a large audience can gauge your knowledge of their industry

- Organize small meetups where entrepreneurs and investors discuss challenges faced by a specific industry

- Organize events, conferences, open houses, or workshops

- Get your voice heard through an active blog and/or social media presence that speaks to your area of expertise and provides practical advice to entrepreneurs

In addition to networking with entrepreneurs, you should meet regularly with other VCs. Yes, some of these VCs might be competition for the best deals, but many of them will be sources for good deal flow and become syndication partners for future investments. Some of the best VCs are willing to act as mentors to new VCs, even if they aren't partners in their own firm. Spend time getting to know other investors and make sure they know what your focus is. If they have a deal outside of their focus area, and they know it is a fit for you, they can refer it. Also, if you are an early stage VC, knowing the top later stage and Corporate VCs is important as you look to help your portfolio companies raise larger rounds of growth stage capital.

And finally, all great VCs have a network of trusted resources they go to for helping out their portfolio companies. In addition to the colleagues you worked with over the years, it's important to build a network that will help you address the many challenges faced by your portfolio companies' early days all the way through to their exits. Our network at Launchpad Venture Group is incredibly diverse. It gives us access to talented people with backgrounds in sales, marketing, engineering, talent development and finance. They've worked in industries such as enterprise software, biotech, medtech, and robotics. They were/are CEOs, CTOs, CFOs, VP Sales & Marketing and many other job titles. So when I need a resource to help one of our CEOs deal with a difficult problem, I know where to go.

In addition to networking with entrepreneurs, you should meet regularly with other VCs. Yes, some of these VCs might be competition for the best deals, but many of them will be sources for good deal flow and become syndication partners for future investments.

Q

What are some of the problems and issues that are specific to a fund which is closely affiliated with another entity such as an Angel Group sidecar fund or an incubator or accelerator fund?

If you are thinking about starting a fund that is closely affiliated with another institution (i.e. a sidecar fund), there are some special considerations to be aware of. In most cases, they can be addressed with specific agreements about operating rules of the road, but not in all cases. Here are some examples of issues to consider, along with a few mitigations that can help.

Angel group sidecar funds are prone to tensions between people using more active and more passive approaches to investing. The angels in groups tend to be more hands-on and active than the investors in the fund (angels who are essentially acting as fund LPs). This difference in approach can create situations where the active investors end up feeling like they are doing all the work while the passive investors are riding their coattails (and the GPs are being paid fees.) This can be addressed through complex mechanisms to pay the active investors for their diligence and company advising efforts. But, that is not always easy. Not only does the value for compensation have to come from somewhere, it can wreak havoc in the group because it starts to convert the best peoples' amateur volunteer "for the love of the game" status into a professional status.

There can also be issues around who should take a board seat - the fund, which is writing a single big check, or one of the more knowledgeable, active small check investors who has been working closely with the company. Closely related to this board seat issue is the question of communications. When someone discovers that the company is having a problem, it can be unclear what the lines of communication are or should be. And, if a problem comes to light after a follow-on round, there can be questions of who knew what when and why they didn't warn others.

Speaking of follow-ons, there can be issues there as well. Investors in the fund might feel angry if individual investors don't follow-on after their initial investments or happen to say critical things about the company. Similarly, individual investors might feel angry and abandoned if the fund chooses, for its own reasons, not to follow-on in a company they supported in the previous round.

Funds affiliated with incubators, accelerators, universities or economic development agencies can present additional tricky problems. To the extent that they are expected to serve an institution, or its alumni, or serve a social purpose such as job creation, they may find that they have some conflict between their non-financial obligations and their drive to achieve the highest possible returns. For example, they may feel obligated to invest in a company because it resides within their organization or to follow-on in a company to keep it alive, when a purely financial investor would have passed on the opportunity.

As you might imagine, some of these issues can be fairly thorny and can lead to some seriously frustrated expectations if they are not mitigated. Not all of these issues can be completely avoided, but there are a few things you can do to try to minimize them:

- Keep the fund independent, if possible, so that it is a closely affiliated "partner" of the institution but able to operate as an independent agent. For example, as a way of ensuring most of the benefits of a tight partnership, without all the drawbacks, you could have a bilateral agreement that not only will the institution share or refer all its companies to the fund on a first refusal basis, but also the fund will agree to make time to scout and maybe advise all of the companies in the institution. This would work somewhat like a right of first review or offer, and thereby create a greater proximity and likelihood of investment, but not an obligation.

- Take time to plot out all the different investing, communicating and decision-making scenarios you can think of that might come up in both the short term and the long term (such as those noted in the special considerations above). Take the time to plan, agree on, and document what the rules will be in each situation. And, because it will not be possible to think of every single scenario, establish a governance mechanism such as a decision-making process, an ethics board or referee who will be the agreed-upon mechanism for guiding behavior in tricky situations.

- Make sure no matter how you set yourself up to run, you painstakingly document and explain your approach to your LPs before they commit their money. At the end of the day, you can run a fund however you want, but you should have a documented plan, and that plan should be clearly explained to your LPs before they invest.

As noted above, venture capital is one of those professions idealized by many and misunderstood by most. To the uninformed, it seems

55

like it should be great, but in actual fact, it is a fairly hard job that is only fit for people with certain temperaments, skills and abilities. Sure, you get to set your own schedule and spend your time doing interesting things, but you really are not your own boss. You are essentially in a service industry, and a very transparent and public one at that. You are a service provider providing investment services to relatively unforgiving LPs who will walk away and never come back if you don't deliver the performance they expect. Not quite as sexy and free-wheeling as many casual observers assume it to be. Still, for the right people, it can be a heck of a ride.

Chapter 4

Strong Foundations: Venture Capital Legal and Accounting - Approaches, Tools and Software

If you make a simple mistake while driving, like hitting some black ice you didn't see, and you skid off the road into a ravine and total your car, assuming no injuries, that's a bummer and a major inconvenience for you. But cleaning the mess up is not super complicated. You need to work with your insurance company to get the car replaced. It's paperwork, but you are the only affected party and you can work through it in a pretty straightforward manner.

But if you borrow your friend's car and do the same thing, sorting out the legalities can be significantly more complicated. Even if the friendship survives, you are going to have to sort it out with two different insurance companies - establish that you had permission to drive the car, that the accident was not negligent or reckless, and that your friend's insurance company (and probably yours too) is on the hook to reimburse your friend up to the limits of the insurance. It is going to be a pain and, unlike the situation where you wreck your own car and have no one to blame but yourself, in this case your friend is affected, and they do have someone to blame: you.

Those same dynamics apply to fund investing. If you lose your money betting on a startup, you have no one to blame but yourself and, assuming no malfeasance on the part of the startup, the legal analysis is not all that complicated. It's whoopsie-daisy and bye-bye money and then you are done. However, if you start an investment fund and collect and lose other people's money, that's a very different story. And guess what? There is no insurance policy in this context to bail you out.

The legal documentation around your fund, and your compliance with its requirements, are the closest thing you've got to insurance. These documents are your only protection for having lost someone else's money. These documents need to make it abundantly clear that your investors (LPs) understood and willingly accepted the risk of loss. They also need to make the terms of that risk acceptance very clear, and your conduct needs to comply with those terms.

Most early stage investors really prefer to avoid mundane tasks related to legal and accounting issues. But when you think of the documentation around your fund through the lens of the car accident analogy, it makes it a bit easier to get motivated. And that's a good thing because, unfortunately, these issues can't be ignored unless you want to end up in jail or slapped with a nasty lawsuit or a large fine. You are taking a ton of risk with other people's money. That is not a trifling matter.

> The legal documentation around your fund, and your compliance with its requirements, are the closest thing you've got to insurance. These documents are your only protection for having lost someone else's money.

The good news is that if you get a little help from competent experts, setting up and managing a venture fund does not have to be too complex from either a legal or an accounting standpoint. Venture funds have been around for many decades, and there are well-defined rules and regulations already in place as well as many advisors who can provide good starting points and walk you through the process. Needless to say, you must engage some good advisors and do what they say!

In this chapter, we will walk you through the main issues related to fund creation, governance and accounting for ordinary stand-alone VC funds. Corporate, university-affiliated, accelerator-affiliated, social impact and government funds are going to have a few additional special provisions and some slightly different issues to contend with, so we will address them separately. Having a good overview of the process and knowing a bit about each of these areas will help you get started, keep your perspective and ask the right questions when you meet with your attorneys and accountants. And, doing it by the book will not only keep you out of hot water with your LPs, it will keep you out of trouble with the S.E.C. and the I.R.S.

One overarching regulatory concept to keep in mind is that a major goal of your fund design will be to ensure that you are not legally considered a mutual fund or hedge fund. Under the Investment Company Act of 1940 ("1940 Act"), mutual funds are extraordinarily tightly regulated in order to protect individual investors. You do not want your fund to be considered a mutual fund. Hedge funds are also tightly regulated because of their potential to wreak havoc on the markets. However, luckily, there is a very workable exemption for venture capital funds (recently further clarified in the Dodd-Frank Wall Street Reform and Consumer Protection Act of 2010) provided they comply with certain guidelines (such as identifying yourself as a VC fund, not holding more than 20% of the fund in one asset, not using debt to fund investments, focusing on private company stocks not public company stocks, and not registering under the 1940 Act). Compliance with these guidelines is not difficult, but it needs to be hardwired into your fund documents. So, at the risk of sounding like a broken record, we will point out again, it is important to have competent experienced counsel and to do what they say!

> The paperwork around a venture fund can appear somewhat intimidating, but the documents are not actually that complicated conceptually.

Q

Christopher, what are the major topics covered by the legal documents that set up a venture fund?

The paperwork around a venture fund can appear somewhat intimidating, but the documents are not actually that complicated conceptually. The fund documents can take the form of a limited liability company ("LLC") operating agreement, a limited liability partnership ("LLP") operating agreement or a more traditional limited partnership agreement. Or they can be a mixture of some or all of the above where an LLC serves as the GP under a traditional partnership agreement. But regardless of the form recommended by your counsel, they are really only going to cover three basic foundational concepts:

1. How the money comes to you

2. What you agree to do with it while you have it

3. How you give the money back to your LPs.

From the 36,000 foot level that's all there really is. You give me money, I invest it, I give you back your principle and some profits and keep a little for myself for my trouble. Of course, each of these concepts involves quite a few underlying nuances, so naturally each is broken down further into quite a few subtopics which map to one or more sections in the fund operating documents. To provide you with some familiarity, we will summarize the primary ones here (leaving some minor ones out in the interests of clarity and brevity). As you are skimming through, keep in mind that each one relates to one of the three main buckets above (money going in, money being used, money going out).

Q

So what are the key sections that virtually all early stage venture fund documents will include?

Corporate and Legal Formalities - This section covers the formation of the fund itself as a legal entity and

related housekeeping issues such as:

- The name of the fund and those of the GPs and LPs

- The fund's offices and addresses

- The designation for an agent for the service of process in the event of a legal dispute

- The form of corporate entity legal residence, and

- The character and purpose of the company.

Capital contributions, membership (or partnership) interests, capital accounts and tax and related matters - Here the documents talk about:

- How and when investors will contribute capital

- How those contributions will translate into legal ownership of a portion of the fund, and

- How that ownership will be recorded and tracked.

There will typically be some language here about taxation of ownership interests earned through profits. And there will usually be some language governing situations where an investor defaults (i.e. does not honor one or more of his/her capital calls to supply funds.)

Profits, losses and distributions - Here is where documents will talk about:

- What the threshold for a profit is

- How ownership of those profits is allocated amongst the members of the fund

- How losses are calculated and allocated, and

- When, and under what circumstances, the General Partners running the fund may or should distribute cash to the investors.

Tax and Regulatory Allocations - Every agreement will have some long and thorny sections relating to handling and accounting for the impacts of various tax and regulatory events. The overall goals of this section are to:

- Maximize tax efficiency,

- Minimize workload for everyone, and

- Ensure the GPs have sufficient authority and flexibility to comply with tax and other regulatory requirements at all time.

So you will see some subsections devoted to tax issues and some of the terminology, borrowed from the tax code, can get extremely jargony and technical including provisions relating to: gross income allocations, loss allocation limitations, adjusted capital account deficits, minimum gain chargebacks, qualified income offsets, non-recourse deductions, fund minimum gain, member non-recourse debt, member non-recourse deductions, reallocations due to I.R.S. adjustments, curative allocations, adjustments upon distribution of property in kind, allocation of capital gains to redeemed members, and tax withholding.

Fiscal Matters - All fund documents will include a section talking about:

- How the books of account will be kept by the GPs

- What the GPs will include in the fund's financial statements

- When they will be submitted to the LPs

- How the GPs will maintain a list of the fund's portfolio holdings, and

- How the GPs will maintain the fund's bank account(s).

Fund Management - Here is where the documents talk about:

- Who the managers are (the GPs)

- What to do if one resigns or is replaced

- What the legal powers and duties of the manager are (i.e. their authority to use their discretion in running the fund, along with their duty of good faith in doing so).

Actions Requiring Consent - This section will outline what decisions require input from the LPs. Typical actions requiring consent would include:

- Making an investment larger than, say, 20% of the fund (which has S.E.C. classification implications)

- Taking on debt, or

- Adding new LPs or taking new money.

Compensation, Fees and Expenses - Here is where the agreement outlines the calculation and handling of the management fees and the fund's other operating expenses.

Manager Conduct - All agreements will have one or more sections talking about:

- Conflicts of interest

- The managers' duty of care

- The use of agents by the managers to represent them

- Contracts with affiliates

- Managers' meetings and decision-making, and

- What degree of business activity outside the fund a manager is permitted to have.

Investors/Members/Partners - Here is where the agreement will talk about:

- The investors in the fund (LPs); for example, whether there is more than one class of LP

- Limitations of liability for members

- Compliance with laws and obligations

- Restrictions on rights of withdrawal of funds

- Tax duties

- Attempted transfers of their LP interests

- Substitutions of a new LP for an existing one, and

- Voting on matters requiring votes.

If you are undertaking to raise a fund of other people's money and invest it into risky startups, and you do not have an airtight indemnification clause, you are playing with fire. It cannot be said more plainly than this: do not do it.

Indemnification - This section is an important one. In legal terms, to indemnify someone is to agree to compensate or make someone whole (or to secure someone against legal liability for their actions) in relation to certain damages under certain conditions. All proper fund documentation will include an indemnification by the fund to the GPs for all their fund decisions and actions taken in good faith. This is really as close as you get to the insurance policy in the borrowed car scenario above. The indemnification section will basically say that the fund will pay the legal liabilities and expenses of the GPs in relation to any issues which arise as a result of their running the fund provided they were acting in good faith and running the fund according to the terms of the fund's documentation. This means the fund is responsible (i.e. the money comes from the fund or its insurers) and that the LPs are not personally liable beyond what they have already put into the fund. If you are undertaking to raise a fund of other people's money and invest it into risky startups, and you do not have an airtight indemnification clause, you are playing with fire. It cannot be said more plainly than this: do not do it.

Redemptions of LP Interests - Most agreements will have a section saying there are no redemptions of interests at an LP's request (i.e. they cannot simply request their money back since it is either invested in or committed to highly illiquid investments), but that there may be mandatory redemptions of an LP's interests by the GPs (i.e. expulsion) if it is in the interest of the fund, or necessary in order to have the fund comply with law or to avoid litigation or claims.

Dissolution of the Fund - This section talks about when it is permissible and/or required to dissolve the fund and what the process of dissolution and distribution of assets, profits and losses will be.

Additional Miscellaneous Legal Clauses - Believe it or not, despite having covered all of the above, there are still a variety of additional topics that most fund documentation will cover. In the miscellaneous section you will find discussion of:

• How the agreements are to be interpreted

• Whether they can be amended

• What state's laws will be applied to them

• What the dispute resolution process will be, and

• How legal notices under the agreement will be given.

As overwhelming as all that sounds, it is really not as difficult as someone unfamiliar with the process might think. If you start to feel overloaded, remember that all of the topics fall into one of those three buckets at the beginning (money going in, money being used, money going out). And keep in mind that good lawyers will walk you through every step of it. In fact, they will likely have a template agreement to start the process and will ask you a series of questions to help them customize it to your needs. If you are patient and respond to uncertainty by asking them clarifying questions about the pros and cons or other implications of a decision, you will find that you can actually move through this quite easily. In fact, compared to fundraising, the documentation is a breeze!

> If you start to feel overloaded, remember that all of the topics fall into one of those three buckets at the beginning (money going in, money being used, money going out).

Q

What restrictions are there on the type and number of investors that can participate in a venture fund?

For the most part, these funds invest in private company deals which are exempt from registration and disclosure requirements under S.E.C. rules (typically the exemption comes under Rule 506). Because these deals are exempt from those registration and disclosure protections, participation in these deals is limited to "accredited investors" only who are deemed by the S.E.C. to be sophisticated enough to evaluate the deal and withstand the loss if necessary. An investor is accredited under S.E.C. rules if he or she has either $200,000 in income or $1,000,000 in net assets excluding the value of the home (higher figures apply to households qualifying jointly.) A fund is accredited only when all the investors in the fund are themselves accredited. So the first requirement is that your LPs must all be accredited investors.

The second main limitation is that, in order to steer clear of the mutual fund rules under the 1940 Act, you are limited in the maximum number of investors you are permitted to have in your fund. As of the time of publication the limit is 99 investors, although the National Venture Capital Association and the Angel Capital Association are part of a coalition that is trying to get that number raised up to 250.

The third limitation is the provisions of S.E.C. Rule 506 which prohibit felons and other "bad actors" from being in any way involved (either on your side as an investor or on the company side) in a deal that is relying on the 506 exemptions above. Most private company investment documents will contain a requirement that investors give a "no bad actor" representation, so as a result, most VC fund documents will contain a parallel "no bad actor" rep so that the fund can sign the investment documents in good faith.

Q

What are the governance standards for a typical venture fund? Are they the same or different than the governance of a portfolio company?

Governance standards for VC funds are totally different than those for portfolio companies. Portfolio companies have an outside board of directors and shareholders. These companies are subject to the statutory law and case law on corporations. In virtually all US states, and especially states like Delaware, this is a huge and richly-developed body of laws and rules that spells out the duties of officers and directors as well as the rights of shareholders.

Much of this law has been built up to protect shareholders who experience a power imbalance because they are at a greater distance from the company than the insiders and must rely on the company for any information they receive. They are essentially at the mercy of the company. So a strong body of law has developed, in

67

every state, around disclosure, fair dealing and protecting the rights of shareholders. Virtually every situation that might go wrong is covered by laws as well as best practices or accepted standards. Failure to apply good governance to a company gives rise to a very serious potential liability to your shareholders.

Venture funds are totally different. They are private partnerships which are negotiated at arm's length by parties who are presumed at law to have pretty equal bargaining power and equal access to information. In effect, in the eyes of the law, the parties are free to arrange whatever private governance terms they can agree on. Neither party is viewed as having an inferior status and neither party is entitled to any special protections. Of course, as with any contractual undertaking, extreme conduct will give rise to a right of remedy. For example, there is plenty of partnership law about fraud, or bad faith between partners, or failing to disclose material terms as part of the agreement, or breach of contract if a partner does not abide by the terms of the agreement. But outside of those extremes the parties are free to use common sense to negotiate terms about how the managers will behave.

> Venture Funds are private partnerships which are negotiated at arm's length by parties who are presumed at law to have pretty equal bargaining power and equal access to information. In effect, in the eyes of the law, the parties are free to arrange whatever private governance terms they can agree on.

As a result, and as noted above, most fund documentation has provisions regarding record keeping, reporting to LPs, and maybe some terms about how investment decisions will be made (by committee, by consensus, by vote, etc.). However, in contrast, it would be rare to see excessive detail on the investment decision-making, and this is for one very common sense reason: the LPs are choosing these GPs entirely because of their good judgement and investing instincts. It would be pointless to intrude in that process with too much in the way of rule-making. Similarly, it is rare to see much language around the fund having its own board of directors, or the GPs having to evaluate each other. The performance speaks for itself and the funds which don't perform don't raise additional money and cease to exist.

Q

What accounting issues does a venture fund manager need to be aware of?

The accounting for funds can get a bit complicated compared to the bookkeeping for a startup. At the most basic level you just need to keep an accurate record of what the fund owns, what its cost basis is, and what its valuation is while also accounting for the costs of running the fund using acceptable accounting standards.

However six realities conspire to really complicate this endeavor:

1. Fund managers need to keep track of which LP owns what percentage of every holding in the fund (based on how much they put into the fund), while making rolling capital calls over the life of the fund;

2. These private company holdings are totally illiquid, have multi-year holding periods until liquidity is reached and are almost impossible to value accurately in the meantime;

3. Different LPs come in at slightly different times (for example the last LP might come in well after the fund has started to invest), so some fair method for allocating the early investments to the later LPs and rebalancing who owns what percentage of the holdings needs to be devised (this is a context in which you'll see terms like net asset value or NAV bandied about);

4. The management fees need to be calculated and deducted from the fund (or at least moved between fund accounts). Rules for

which portions of fund money is subject to management fees, and for how long, tend to be relatively complicated because LPs don't want to overpay fees or create perverse incentives;

5. The calculation of GP "carry" or share of profits can be fairly complicated for reasons having to do with hurdle rates (to ensure that LPs are paid back all their capital before GPs are paid anything) and the need for repeatedly updating valuations of holdings, exit proceeds held in escrow in portfolio company mergers and acquisitions, lock-ups and holding periods in the context of IPOs, and situations where portfolio companies have not yet been sold at the end of the fund and need to be distributed in kind to LPs; and, finally,

6. All this needs to be done in the most convenient and tax-efficient manner possible so that income and taxes on that income are as closely matched as possible (so for example, someone does not have imputed tax on phantom income but no actual cash

income to pay the tax). And in a perfect world, any losses incurred by the fund could be passed through and used by LPs as they are incurred.

Ideally you will get some good tax advice while you are designing the fund so that the fund structure and documents are tax-optimized and the rules of the road on accounting and allocating are clear and fair to all. And then as you are working with all these rules, you will want to be transparently reporting (see Chapter 7) what is going on to your LPs through regular quarterly statements and annual financial reports.

Q

Do you have any advice on how to find good legal and accounting services for a new fund manager? And, what do you think is a reasonable range in costs for these services?

You want experienced lawyers. But the key to selecting good lawyers is to understand exactly what it means to "be experienced". This is more than just a question of whether they are the right kind of lawyer: a corporate lawyer, as opposed to, say, an environmental lawyer. To be good and efficient at your transaction, they have to have actually done this exact type of transaction before. Otherwise you are going to be paying them to learn on your dime as they go along. And, more importantly, lawyers unfamiliar with this kind of transaction are inevitably going to miss issues that should have been spotted when "a stitch in time could save nine". In a perfect world, they would have done this kind of transaction for the same "side" in the past: representing the licensor of software is different than the licensee; representing the buyer of a company is different than representing the seller. So if you can have your pick of lawyers, you are looking for someone who has formed funds like this for GPs like you in the past. You want to make sure they work closely with a team of tax law specialists to ensure their document templates (and any changes you request) are up to

spec with respect to current tax rules.

So if you can have your pick of lawyers, you are looking for someone who has formed funds like this for GPs like you in the past. You want to make sure they work closely with a team of tax law specialists to ensure their document templates (and any changes you request) are up to spec with respect to current tax rules.

The legal cost of setting up a fund can range anywhere from $10,000 to $100,000 depending on the size, complexity, degree of customization and the city in which you are doing it (big city law practices tend to have more specialized expertise, but also higher hourly billing rates). Keep in mind, however, that trying to economize by seeking out lower billing rates may not actually save you money in the long run. Often the more expensive, but deeply experienced and very time-efficient senior practitioner is going to end

71

up being cheaper in terms of doing the initial work more efficiently. And, their expertise may save you mistakes which end up being very costly down the road.

Finding good accounting help is somewhat easier because the work involves reasonably straightforward partnership and LLC pass-through taxation issues with which most decent-sized practices will be familiar. But here as well, paying for experience can save you money. More experienced partners have seen the traps and pitfalls before and can anticipate the key issues and help you plan for them. And keep in mind that a very big part of your cost is going to be up front in getting the tax and accounting practitioners up to speed on the terms and details of your fund and getting the fund data (such as holdings, allocations and LP addresses) loaded into their system. So you want to pick a good quality firm with a long-standing reputation and a relatively deep bench of talent. Outgrowing your firm or having to switch due to performance issues will require you to incur the start-up costs all over

again. In terms of annual fees, again it will depend on the size and complexity of your fund (including the number of LPs), but you are looking at a range of about $2,500 per year to as much as $15,000 per year for more complex funds.

One budgetary planning item worth mentioning is that shutting down your fund at its conclusion is often not a trivial matter. If all your companies are not exited, it may be necessary to amend the operating agreements to extend the length of the fund beyond its original 10 years, which means getting amended papers re-signed by all the LPs. And even then you may find that you have to wind down with as yet un-exited holdings, which can mean finding a buyer for your holdings or distributing the stock to LPs in-kind on a pro-rata basis. Both of these sorts of transactions can be very messy and burn up a lot of time from legal, accounting and tax professionals. Expect shutting down your fund to cost roughly as much as starting it up. And then afterwards there will still be one, or possibly two, trailing tax filings when you are done.

Q

What about the tools you use to manage your venture fund portfolios? Is Excel good enough for venture fund management, or do you have a better solution to take on this challenge?

When I first started investing many years ago, I found Excel to be good enough to manage a small number of investments. As time went by and the size of my portfolio grew, I started to run into a number of portfolio management challenges. I would say that my biggest challenges fell into the following areas:

- **Portfolio Valuation**: Keeping track of convertible notes, warrants and preferred stock, new rounds of financing, etc. made it very difficult to accurately calculate the value of my portfolio and track KPIs (Key Performance Indicators) such as DPI (Distributed to Paid-In) and TVPI (Total Value to Paid-In).

- **Tax Records**: Pulling together all of my prior year transaction records for my accountant

became cumbersome and time consuming.

- **Reporting**: Quarterly and Annual Reports for my LPs required days of tedious work, and came at the expense of helping my portfolio companies succeed.

- **Analysis**: Although Excel does have some basic graphing and charting, I didn't have good visualization tools to help me analyze my portfolio in a convenient dashboard.

- **Accessibility**: I spend much of my time on the road which makes reviewing an Excel spreadsheet on a smartphone very difficult. I needed a tool that was mobile friendly.

To address those challenges, Ham and I decided we needed to move on from Excel. When we researched portfolio management platforms, we found nothing that met our needs. Having spent most of our careers in the software industry, we launched our own startup and set out to build a powerful portfolio management solution to address the challenges of managing and valuing venture investments. Today we use Seraf to track the Launchpad group portfolio, as well as our personal portfolios and all three of the funds we operate. Thousands of angels, VCs, family offices, accelerators and angel groups around the world have joined us, making Seraf the leader in early stage portfolio management.

> Properly designing and running a venture capital fund is actually a fairly complex endeavor that requires mastery over many legal, accounting and tax concepts. With help and advice from experts these concepts can be mastered well enough to get your fund up and running.

Although the people who claim venture capital is a totally unregulated business are pretty much correct, this is not the same as saying it is a simple business. Properly designing and running a venture capital fund is actually a fairly complex endeavor that requires mastery over many legal,

accounting and tax concepts. With help and advice from experts these concepts can be mastered well enough to get your fund up and running, but even then there will be very significant ongoing accounting, reporting and tax filing work. That is the reality of the VC business. LPs are sophisticated and there is nothing informal about this industry. This reality should not scare away people who believe they are well-suited for the work, but it must be appreciated so that would-be fund managers understand what they are getting themselves into before quitting their day job.

Chapter 5

Key Success Factors: Essential Skills for Every VC Fund Team

About five years ago, Ham and I were approached by an old friend of Ham's with a new concept for a venture fund. This friend was a recently retired partner at a top tier VC firm based in Boston. After attending a meeting of our angel group, Launchpad, he was struck by how our group operated. In particular, he was intrigued by the process we use when companies pitch to our membership.

At Launchpad, companies give a 15 minute pitch followed by a 10 minute Q&A session. Next, we ask the entrepreneur to leave the room and our group discusses the presentation around small tables of 6 to 8 people. After a 10 minute discussion, we ask each table to select a spokesperson. This individual gives a quick synopsis of what her table liked about the company followed by any questions or concerns they had during their round table discussion.

The end result of this process is a time-efficient crowdsourcing of a concise list of the key topics to cover during a due diligence process as observed by a large group with a very broad experience and skill base. My friend was struck by how different this approach was for a company pitch versus the deal pitching process at his previous venture firm. He was most impressed by the resources and breadth of perspectives we had access to through Launchpad members.

He immediately began to think about building a new kind of venture fund. Instead of relying on just one or two partners to help him evaluate potential investments, he envisioned a hybrid model with traditional GPs but also leveraging the talents of Launchpad's roster of 150 investors. According to his plan, the three of us would act as the main General Partners (GPs) and the group would be a fourth GP for a $150M fund. Certainly, this was a novel structure for a venture firm with a fund of that size. Unfortunately, we don't know whether our fund would have worked or not since, for a variety of personal, professional and economic climate issues, we chose not to go forward with the idea.

Here we are five years later, and we are starting to see venture firms build variations on this type of structure -- a few core GPs supported by a large network of experienced executives, entrepreneurs or investors. Venture capital is a challenging industry in which to be successful. It relies on a lot of hard work, thoughtful analysis and investor judgement by a relatively small team. Surrounding your core team with additional experienced talent could play a critical role in your long term success, so the temptation toward this kind of structure is obvious. With that story as a preamble, let's take a closer look at that core team at the center of things. What are the people skills and resources you need to build a long term, sustainable venture capital firm?

Q

Ham, you've run a couple of funds as a GP and worked with dozens of venture capital firms over the years. What are some of the key skills you expect to see in the GPs at a successful firm?

Let's start by focusing on the major components of a VC's day-to-day job. What follows isn't an exhaustive list, but it does cover the major job responsibilities.

- Raising capital for your fund from Limited Partners (LPs)

- Finding great companies to invest in

- Doing thorough due diligence on potential investments

- Negotiating and syndicating deals

- Helping your portfolio companies succeed

So with that list as an anchoring point, let's discuss the primary set of skills needed by a VC.

A great VC anticipates and understands market trends. As a forward thinker, it's not easy being ahead of the pack. Many of your investments will be too early (i.e. your market timing was off) or derailed by other market forces.

Raising capital for your fund from Limited Partners: Unless your venture fund has a captive source of capital, such as you and your partners' personal funds, a corporate sponsor or a government sponsor, you will end up spending a fair amount of time and travel dollars pitching to many potential LPs. Any good salesperson knows how to qualify potential customers, pitch their product and close a deal. The process works pretty much the same for VCs raising money from LPs. So make sure at least one person on your venture team knows what it takes to sell and knows how to close the sale!

Finding great companies to invest in: Venture capital is all about investing in the future. You are betting on teams today to create things that are going to matter 7-10 years in the future. A great VC anticipates and understands market trends. As a forward thinker, it's not easy being ahead of the pack. Many of your investments will be too early (i.e. your market timing was off) or derailed by other market forces. You have to be a big picture thinker and comfortable making decisions without a lot of supporting data as you judge long term market potential for new ideas.

Doing thorough due diligence on potential investments: Comprehensive diligence on a startup company requires a fair amount of effort. Once you have satisfied yourself that the big picture frame of reference justifies further work, you need to shift gears and get down into the nitty gritty and try to spot issues that might be deal killers. You will cover topics such as viability of the technology, size of market opportunity, competition, go-to-market strategy, financial plan, etc. Even with all of those analytical aspects requiring thorough research, we believe the most important aspect of diligence ends up being more subjective. In many ways your most important assessment relates to evaluating the CEO and her management team. The quality of the founding team is perhaps the biggest factor in startup success. Another key, often overlooked, skill relates to your ability to be decisive and make important decisions quickly. There's nothing worse for the entrepreneur than having a VC string them along and not pull the trigger on either a quick yes or no. Slow decision making will hurt your reputation in the venture community and may cost you deals lost to your faster competitors.

> An often overlooked skill relates to your ability to be decisive and make important decisions quickly. There's nothing worse for the entrepreneur than having a VC string them along and not pull the trigger on either a quick yes or no.

Negotiating and syndicating deals: This role requires a few important skills. First off, you need to understand how venture investments are structured from a financial standpoint. When you negotiate an investment with an early stage company, valuation is only one of many variables to consider. Envisioning a long term funding strategy for the company and making sure you are in alignment with the management team and co-investors on potential exit strategies is vitally important. Solid skills in venture finance are at

the core of a successful VC's DNA. Another key skill in this role relates to your ability to sell to both entrepreneurs and other venture investors. By this, we mean your ability to come to a fair agreement with the company on deal terms, and where appropriate, syndicate the deal with other investors to help fill out the financing round.

Helping your portfolio companies succeed: Startups find new ways to fail every day. As a VC, you have to accept company failure as part of the job. But, that doesn't mean you should sit on the sidelines and pray for success. Hope is not a strategy! VCs need to be active partners with their portfolio companies. Frequently, they take board seats where they add value to the company. Great board members have an ability to provide guidance and support without the ego-driven need to control or dictate everything. And, their prior business experience should help a company make decisions that lead to success. Not everyone is cut out to be an effective contributor to a startup board. These are some of the most important skills and personal characteristics for a board member:

- Temperament — calm and experienced, good perspective

- Independent thinker — questions and pushes back

- Proactive — involved by initiating regular interaction with CEO

- Committed — willing to put in the time

- Networked — offers help and support by leveraging their personal network

- Strategic — focuses on strategy, not tactics

- Thoughtful & Observant — first to spot issues or notice what is missing

- Informed — insists on good practices and knows the rules of the road

- Supportive — provides mentorship, skill development and the opportunity to lead.

When it comes to fast moving startups, you cannot afford to take your eye off the ball. "Business as usual" is never good enough – companies grow and change quickly — the investor's job is to step back and always consider the bigger picture, speak up and ask questions, and offer perspective and advice.

Another key skill in this role relates to your ability to sell to both entrepreneurs and other venture investors. By this, we mean your ability to come to a fair agreement with the company on deal terms, and where appropriate, syndicate the deal with other investors to help fill out the financing round.

Q

What's the right number of partners at a venture firm?

Well, that depends on a variety of factors such as fund size, target portfolio size, number of expected board seats, and expectations regarding per-partner fee and carry income. You need enough partners to be able to manage the workload and cover a broad experience base, but not so many partners that decision-making and meeting scheduling are cumbersome and per-partner income is diluted beyond an acceptable level. That said, we believe that even for a very small fund, it's wise to have at least two GPs. Even the most talented individual will be weak in a few of the skills we discuss above or weak on the administrative details of running a fund. In addition, most potential LPs are looking for some bench strength on the team and won't want to invest in a single GP.

Another common configuration on a venture fund team is to have one founding GP with one or more Managing Directors and/or Venture Partners to help run the fund. How you build out your team and establish job titles is up to you as a founding partner. Just make sure everyone is clear on their roles and responsibilities.

Q

What other personnel resources are needed within a successful venture firm?

Fund economics will drive some of your decisions on what resources you can afford to help manage your fund. A small firm with less than $20M under management might choose to have the GPs do all the work with the exception of legal, tax and accounting related tasks that are best handled by outside professional firms. For firms with bigger budgets, there are a variety of positions that need filling.

Analysts: For larger funds, recent college graduates and MBA program graduates are great resources for doing a lot of the grunt work that every firm has to take on. Responsibilities taken on

81

by these junior team members typically include a variety of tasks such as industry research, deal sourcing and screening, due diligence, financial analysis and fund reporting. GPs will maintain their involvement in these tasks, but it's always good to have a helping hand to ease the burden. If you plan to stretch your dollars by using younger lower salaried analysts, you should remember that analysts are often long on MBA theory and short on actual experience, so they are best used in decision-supporting roles rather than decision-making roles.

Finance and Administrative: Managing a venture firm's growing portfolio along with managing the business of the firm can become a significant job over time. Portfolio management involves tracking your fund's investments, staying on top of your capital allocation strategy, reviewing investment legal documents, sending funds to portfolio companies, collecting capital calls, reporting results to LPs on a regular basis and calculating and distributing proceeds as the fund winds down. Managing the

firm's business includes all of the usual tasks controlled by the finance department in almost any type of company. With all of these finance related duties, many venture firms hire a part- or full-time CFO.

Marketing: With more and more sources of financing available to entrepreneurs, getting your firm's name and reputation out in the market is critical. Many VCs use social media and web publishing as vehicles for marketing their firm to entrepreneurs, LPs and other VCs. Just because it's easy to set up a blog or twitter account and start writing, doesn't mean your message will be heard. Venture funds need to build brand awareness just like any other company. Having marketing resources to help you build your brand and using social media alongside other marketing programs are much needed in today's competitive environment.

Advisors: In the introduction to this chapter, we tell a story about building a venture firm with close ties to a large angel group. Having a large, talented pool of experienced entrepreneurs at your side gives you a critical edge in many dimensions. Your advisor network should help you to source deals, perform diligence and help portfolio companies succeed. They won't do all this for free, but compensating them based on some of the carry from your fund should be sufficient motivation. It takes significant time on the part of the GPs to manage this resource, but it's time well spent when you can keep them active and engaged.

> There are few types of work which require a smaller team to cover a wider swath of competencies than venture capital.

Suffice it to say, there are few types of work which require a smaller team to cover a wider swath of competencies than venture capital. Good VCs tend to be very well-rounded people, drawing on skills typically associated with each end of the introversion/extroversion scale. VCs need the networking, communicating, people-skills kinds of traits which tend to be attributed to extroverts. And, they need those analytical, detail-oriented, self-guided, independent thinker kinds of traits which tend to be attributed to introverts. The team approach can help balance people out, but only to a limited degree. For reasons having to do with fund economics, teams tend to be relatively small. And for reasons having to do with accountability and ownership of one's own outcomes, each VC tends to run his or her own deals from inception to exit. So it is work that realistically only suits a subset of people. Put another way, while virtually all very successful VCs tend to be pretty smart, well-rounded and accomplished people, not all smart well-rounded and accomplished people are meant to be VCs!

Chapter 6

Dividing the Pie: How Venture Fund Economics Work

Before we dive into the details on how the economics work on an early stage venture fund, let's cut right to the chase. Running an early stage venture fund is not an easy way to get rich quick. In fact, it's probably the most amount of work for the least amount of income in the world of private equity.

Early stage venture funds tend to be small in scale which means the compensation is necessarily small in scale. A typical early stage fund will have less than $100M in assets under management versus $1B+ for later stage private equity funds. Compensation to fund General Partners (GPs) grows with scale. And that's one big reason why most successful VCs and private equity professionals attempt to raise larger and larger amounts of capital each time they raise new funds. It's all about the big payday, and bragging rights at the country club!

Don't get me wrong, with a couple lucky outcomes, you can make good money with a small venture fund, but you won't be buying a private jet with your profits. Before you devote the next 10+ years of your life to raising a venture fund and then managing the fund to its end-of-life, it helps to understand how the economics of a fund work for the GPs. With this chapter we will discuss a range of topics, including management fees, carry, GP commitments, fund expenses and expected financial outcomes on funds that range from middle of

the pack returns to top quartile returns.

Q

Ham, can you explain the two key components of compensation in a venture fund -- management fees and carry?

Let's start with the **management fee**. This is an annual fee that covers the salaries and organizational expenses of a venture firm. A typical early stage fund will charge an annual management fee of around 2%. This fee is based on the total amount of capital committed to the fund and typically applies only to the portion of the money that has been put to work. In the case of a $50M fund, the management fee will be 2% of that total, which works out to a theoretical maximum of $1M annually assuming the entire fund was invested.

In most cases, this level of management fee will be in place for a limited time period. For example it might just apply for the first 5 years of the fund. This is the time period in which new investments are made and most of the follow-on investments occur. After the first 5 years, the 2% fee is usually based on the remaining invested capital (i.e. the amount of capital the fund has invested in active companies in the portfolio.) Over the life of this $50M fund, the fund will pay out in the neighborhood of $7.5M in management fees. That represents 15% of the fund's original committed capital.

What is the right percentage for a management fee? Should it be 2%? It depends on a number of factors. For very small funds, say $20M in size, a 2% fee results in a $400K annual management fee. That should be enough to meet your fund's organizational expenses and pay very modest salaries to the GPs. But, in small funds, it's not unusual for the management fee to be a bit higher at 2.5%, reflecting the extra work associated with investing in the smallest deals and youngest companies. The converse is true for large funds. At $1B in size, a large venture fund would pay out $20M in annual management fees. In that case, you might see management fees set closer to 1.5%, or if set at 2%, subject to more time or other restrictions.

The management fee on a small venture fund will help you keep the lights on and pay your bills, but you won't get rich on those fees. The real returns for a VC come from the profits paid out on the overall returns from your investments. A percentage of a fund's profits are paid to the GPs, and this payment is called **carry or carried interest**. This percentage tends to vary between 15% and 30% for most venture funds, with 20% being typical, and lower carry associated with higher fee funds and higher carry associated with low fee or no fee funds.

> The management fee on a small venture fund will help you keep the lights on and pay your bills, but you won't get rich on those fees. The real returns for a VC come from the profits paid out on the overall returns from your investments.

Before a fund pays out a dollar of carry to the GPs, it must first return all of the capital committed by the LPs. Let's explain this concept using the following example.

- We raise $50M for our venture fund, and set the carry at 20%

- After 5 years, a portfolio company is acquired and the fund gets $40M returned

- The entire $40M will go to the LPs and the fund returns 80% of their capital

- Soon after, another company is acquired and we get $20M returned to the fund

- Of that $20M, the fund returns $10M to the LPs

- The fund has now returned all of the original $50M to the investors

- The remaining $10M will be divided as follows: 80% to the LPs and 20% to the GPs

- That means $8M goes to the LPs and $2M goes to the GPs

- Once the capital return "hurdle" has been reached, any capital returned to the fund through future exits will be distributed to the LPs and GPs using this same 80/20 split.

Here's one final note on the level of management fees and carry. If you are a new VC, it can be difficult to raise a first time fund. It's not unusual for an LP who becomes your anchor investor to ask for better terms than the rest of your LPs. In exchange for the reduced fees, this anchor LP will make introductions to other potential LPs and help you market the fund to raise your desired level of capital. That will save you a ton of time and is probably worth the reduction in your overall compensation from the fund. Similarly, it is not unusual for new GPs (or very aggressive established VCs) to offer to forego fees and take all their compensation in the form of (a higher rate of) carry so that in effect they are putting their money where their mouth is and not asking to be paid as money managers unless they actually generate a profit.

Q

What level of capital commitment to a venture fund do LPs expect from the GPs?

Reading between the lines, what you are really asking is how much skin in the game should each GP have in the fund? If I am an LP, I want to know that all of the GPs are going to be working hard to make sure the fund is a success. If the GPs are making a lot of money from management fees, that doesn't work for me. I want their motivation to be strongly aligned with my expectation for top quartile returns from a venture fund.

With that said, GP commitment is typically in the low single digits because, unlike the LPs who are often representing third parties and institutional money, this money is coming out of personal GP funds. Even at moderate fund sizes these low single digit percentages can add up quickly. In the past, the GP commitment for most funds was in the 1%+ range. So, for example, with a $100M fund, the GPs would be expected to contribute $1M. If

you have four GPs on a fund of that size, the capital commitment works out to $250K for each GP. For a new venture firm with young GPs, that might represent a significant amount of their personal investable assets.

A GP's capital commitment to the fund is typically in the low single digits because, unlike the LPs who are often representing third parties and institutional money, this money is coming out of personal GP funds.

Let's look at another example. Suppose the GPs are entrepreneurs who cashed out big time from a previous startup they founded. If their net worth is north of $50M each, and they are only committing $250K, they don't have enough riding on the line. In a scenario like that, LPs might expect their capital commitment to be more like 10% of the fund, but in return, the GPs might request more carry to reflect their proprietary experience and connections.

Q

What level of investment returns do LPs expect from a venture fund?

Because the risks of investing in startup companies are much greater than the risks of investing in public companies, and the holding periods are long, the fees are significant, and the money is totally tied up and illiquid throughout, VC funds need to outperform the public stock market indices (S&P 500, NASDAQ 100, etc.) by a significant amount to make economic sense. So an annual 10% rate of return for an investor in a VC fund is not enough. LPs are looking for annual return percentages at least in the high teens or low twenties. Or put another way, they are looking for 5-15 percentage points above what the money would have done in a broad-based market index during the same period. And keep in mind that the effective performance threshold is raised by the fact that GPs are taking management fees out as they go along, and also ultimately taking a carry out of any profits.

This means GPs have to exceed those levels of return on a gross basis to ensure they meet the performance expectations of the LPs on a net-of-fees-and-carry basis.

Based on detailed research from Cambridge Associates, the top quartile of VC funds have an average annual return ranging from 15% to 27% over the past 10 years, compared to an average of 9.9% S&P 500 return per year for each of those ten years.

So, if you are an investor in one of these top quartile funds, your returns are better than what you would expect to achieve in the public market indices. However, if you invested in one of the bottom quartile VC funds over the past 10 years, your returns are mostly in the low single digits. You would have been better off in a fund that tracks the S&P 500 (and you would have paid a lot less in fees)! And, not surprisingly, there has been much written about how the average VC fund has underperformed relative to expectations and various benchmarks. This is a hard business and the only thing that keeps the

LPs coming back is the promise of outsized returns that might be achieved if they end up in one of the top performing funds.

In addition to analyzing annual rates of return, it's helpful and common for LPs evaluating VC funds to look at the Distributed to Paid-In (DPI) ratio and the Total Value to Paid-In (TVPI) ratio.

- The DPI ratio is a calculation of the total amount of capital returned to the investors divided by the amount of capital invested into the fund.

- The TVPI ratio is a calculation of the total amount of capital returned to the investors along with any remaining value still in the fund divided by the amount of capital invested into the fund.

It should be noted, if you want to be a top decile fund, your final DPI ratio needs to be around 3x. In other words, for every 1 dollar invested in a VC fund, there needs to be a return to LPs of 3 dollars over the subsequent 10 year time period. As you can see in the Cambridge Associates chart below, the TVPI ratio (light blue bars), goes as high as 4.5x in the boom years of the Internet bubble and down to 1.5x during the post-bubble years.

Upper Quartile Fund Performance 1995-2015

91

Taken together these VC performance indices should give early stage investors a sense of what the professional money managers achieve when working with these startup companies (albeit at a slightly later stage.)

> If you want to be a top decile fund, your final DPI ratio needs to be around 3x. In other words, for every 1 dollar invested in a VC fund, there needs to be a return to LPs of 3 dollars over the subsequent 10 year time period.

Q

What are some ways to improve the rate of return for the LPs?

As discussed in the question above, the Internal Rate of Return (IRR), also known as the Annual Rate of Return, for a venture fund should be in the 15% to 27% range. There are approaches that GPs can look at to help improve the IRR results for

their LPs. To understand how GPs might apply these approaches to their fund, it is important to understand key factors that affect your annual rate of return. Computing your fund's IRR is all about tracking the timing as well as the inflows and outflows of money. This can be a rather labor-intensive thing to do manually with a spreadsheet, but fund management platforms like Seraf will do this for you automatically, which can greatly speed up and improve the quality of your reporting to LPs. The longer amount of time your fund keeps the LP's money, the lower the IRR is for the LP.

To understand this concept, let's use a simple example. Which of the following two investments would you rather have?

1) You get 4X your original investment in 2 years

2) You get 8X your original investment in 6 years

Many would reflexively jump for the 8X. But I would go with investment 1, because I am doubling my money every year. With investment 2, you are doubling your money

92

every 2 years. The time and risk horizon on the second investment is longer, and, of course, so is the opportunity cost you would incur by tying your money up in it. Simple though it is, this example shows you the importance of time when it comes to annual rates of investment returns.

So, if GPs wish to use this approach to improve LP returns, they need to **carefully manage the timing and flow of money into the fund**. In venture funds, it is common practice to make multiple capital calls during the early years of the fund's life cycle. Some funds will ask for 33% of the committed capital at the launch of the fund, followed by two additional 33% capital calls during the early years of the fund's life. That keeps things simple and efficient for the GPs and ensures that cash is readily available when you need to move quickly to make an investment in one of your portfolio companies. However, it's not an efficient use of your LPs' capital. In an ideal world, you would only make capital calls for the exact amount of cash you need at the exact time it's needed. That way,

your LPs keep their cash in their own accounts. But that is an extreme and you are going be looking for a balance. By adopting a program of more frequent, smaller capital calls, a venture fund can boost it's IRR for the LPs by a few percentage points (in exchange for additional fund management work).

Another option for improving fund returns relates to **lowering the payout percentage of management fees**. This approach to boosting returns won't work for many GPs because it results in lower income during the early years of the fund. But for those GPs who can afford to forgo near term income, it's an interesting option.

Here's an example of how it works:

In our $50M fund example, a 2% management fee will result in $7.5M paid out in management fees. Those fees reduce the amount of capital available for investments to $42.5M because the fees come out of the committed capital. If you want to show your LPs that you have real skin in the game, what better way than to invest those management fees with the fund and thereby boost the actual size of the fund's holdings while reducing your up-front take home management fee in exchange for more of your upside on the success of the fund! This approach gives the fund more money in the winners to base their calculated returns on, and it shows LPs how confident the GPs are in the fund that they will invest their fees alongside rather than take them up front.

Q

What are some of the costs associated with running a fund and who pays for these organizational expenses?

The annual management fee for a venture firm is designed to be used to pay the operational expenses associated with running the fund. These expenses include some or all of the following items:

- Salaries and benefits for the GPs

- Salaries and benefits for other employees (e.g. venture partners,

analysts, office managers, CFO, etc.)

- Rent and operating expenses for an office

- Marketing programs to raise the visibility of the fund to entrepreneurs, syndicate partners and LPs

- Legal and accounting fees

- Travel related to sourcing deals, attending board meetings and industry events

- Annual meetings to keep your LPs informed and engaged

- Software (e.g. portfolio management, CRM, accounting)

So that 2% management fee has a lot of mouths to feed and bills to pay. All those expenses can make a $1M management fee from a $50M fund not seem so lucrative after all! As a side note, in the process of forming a new fund, significant costs are incurred related to the marketing and legal setup of the fund. There are some cases where these startup expenses are paid on a pro-rata basis by the LPs.

Another source of expense occurs when a fund uses outside advisors to help source, evaluate and advise portfolio companies. These advisors can be paid in a variety of ways, but most often are paid through a share of the GP carry and some cash from the annual management fees.

> So that 2% management fee has a lot of mouths to feed and bills to pay. All those expenses can make a $1M management fee from a $50M fund not seem so lucrative after all!

Q

In addition to receiving compensation from management fees and carry, should VCs expect to receive compensation if they take a board seat on a portfolio company?

Here's a typical structure for an early stage board:

- 1 or 2 from the Management Team: CEO and a co-founder
- 1 or 2 Investor(s)
- 1 or 2 Independent Director(s)

For the management directors, compensation practice is typically just their ordinary compensation and bonus plan and perhaps participation in the company's option plan (since they likely already have a lot of founder stock.) For independent directors, it is typical to give options or restricted stock units totaling 0.25%-1.5% of the company. But when it comes to the investor board seats, compensation can vary by type of investor. It is not uncommon for individual angels to be paid modest compensation in the form of stock. However, the VC investor component of the board is a bit different for a few reasons:

- First, they appointed themselves by contractual right
- Second, they are already major shareholders by way of their fund, and
- Third, in the case of VCs, they are already being paid a management fee, and some carry

for duties like board service. It's their day job.

For these reasons, it's unlikely that a VC will get additional stock in a company through board compensation. Furthermore, in some fund agreements, any compensation received through board director fees may ultimately reduce the annual management fee paid to the fund. Bottom line… don't expect to boost your income through board compensation.

Q

So with all we discussed above, what level of compensation can a VC make running an early stage venture fund?

There are numerous factors that drive overall compensation for a VC in a venture fund. Let's take a quick look at each of these factors and then we can run a few example cases to see what range of compensation a VC can expect from an early stage fund.

- **Fund Size**: Are you running a $10M, $50M or $100M fund?

- **Management Fee**: Is your fee typical at 2% or are there other factors such as a lower fee for an anchor LP?

- **Carry**: Is your carry typical at 20%?

- **Fund Returns**: Was your fund a top performing fund returning 3X committed capital or did you underperform and end up close to 1.5X?

- **Number of GPs**: Is the firm run by 2 GPs who split the carry evenly or do you have more GPs along with venture partners and advisors who receive some of the carry?

These five factors are the single biggest contributors to overall compensation for a VC. For small funds managing under $20M, the operating expenses of the fund (e.g. rent, employees, advisor fees, etc.) can eat up a substantial portion of the annual management fee. In that situation, the majority of the VC's compensation comes from the carry driven by strong fund performance.

96

In the table below, we will run through a few examples that are based on the five key factors listed above. In order to simplify the exercise, we will make some assumptions, including:

- Half the management fee goes to overhead and half is paid to GPs

- The management fee is set at 7.5% of committed capital over the 10 years life of the fund

- The fund is run by 3 GPs who split the carry and remaining management fee evenly

- Carry is set at 20%

- The LPs contribute 100% of the fund's capital - no capital comes from the GPs

Finally, we will look at three fund sizes: $10M, $50M and $100M, and those funds will either return 1.5X or 3X. Please note: the payouts listed in the table are based on the compensation paid per GP over the full 10 years of the fund.

Let's take a closer look at these numbers. In the first scenario where a $10M fund returns 1.5X of capital, each GP will earn $125,000 in management fees over the 10 year fund life and will be paid an additional $333,333 in carry. Over the full 10 years of the fund, each GP makes approximately $450K, or $45K per year and that is an average - in the early years they will make nothing. In the scenario where this $10M fund returns 3X of

Fund Size & Return	Management Fee	Carry	Total 10 Yr Compensation per GP
$10M returns 1.5X	$125,000	$333,333	$458,333
$10M returns 3X	$125,000	$1,333,333	$1,458,333
$50M returns 1.5X	$625,000	$1,666,667	$2,291,667
$50M returns 3X	$625,000	$6,666,667	$7,291,667
$100M returns 1.5X	$1,250,000	$3,333,333	$4,583,333
$100M returns 3X	$1,250,000	$13,333,333	$14,583,333

invested capital, the GPs make approximately $145K per year. Doesn't look like you are going to get rich managing a $10M fund.

Now let's look at the best case scenario from this table. A $100M fund that returns 3X of invested capital will pay out $14.5M to each of the GPs over the 10 year life of the fund. Now it's starting to get interesting! Average annual compensation exceeds $1M, but remember, most of that compensation will come in the latter years of the fund as companies exit and carry gets distributed.

> Performance tends to get rewarded, and there are no real shortcuts or ways to get rich quick.

To help you dig into venture fund compensation and allow you to play around with key assumptions, we've built a modeling tool (See the Appendix) that you can adjust and build scenarios with. We designed this tool to allow you to factor in the five major assumptions on venture compensation along with some of the other factors that will drive your results.

As you contemplate some of the foregoing material, I am sure you are realizing that the VC fund business is not all that different from other areas in life. Performance tends to get rewarded, and there are no real shortcuts or ways to get rich quick. This is not intended to be discouragement. Fund work is some of the most interesting work a person can do, and may have tremendous ancillary benefits with impact funds or affiliated funds. And, if it turns out that you are good at it and have a little luck, you might find that the leverage inherent in the structures of this industry end up compensating you very handsomely indeed. So by all means, if you think it might be fit for you, give it your best shot!

Chapter 7

Information Flow: Essentials of Venture Capital Fund Reporting

A number of years ago Christopher and I were amongst a group of investors who funded a clever young entrepreneur with an interesting hardware-enabled software platform. As a somewhat informal "company-led" round, let alone one by a consumer device company focused on a leisure activity, the round was not the kind of deal we would normally be attracted to. But we really liked the CEO and thought he was unusually capable, charismatic and action-oriented. The technology and software combination seemed very differentiated, even if the initial target market was a little on the small side.

So a bunch of us decided to back him. Most of us had some general familiarity with aspects of the business - building SaaS platforms, manufacturing basics, mobile apps, etc. But no one was a true expert on this kind of device, the precise demographic being served, or this company's particular retail channel. And given it was a company-led round with no real lead, there was no easy way to put someone on the board, and no obvious expert to select even if there had been a way.

People shrugged and viewed it as one of those small seed rounds where the company uses a bit of early money to make some progress and de-risk itself and then raises a proper round with a good deal lead and all the normal protections and bells and whistles. What could possibly go wrong?

Well, experienced investors can probably guess how things played out. As time went by, it became clear to some of the investors who were a little closer to the company that the CEO was swamped and likely in over his head. These investors heard rumors of one-off problems such as small design and manufacturing issues, slow progress with marketing partners, and bugs in the software algorithms. But most of what trickled out to the investors was just rumors or casual responses to inquiries when investors happened to ask or run into the CEO around town.

Eventually, given the lack of experience and controls, and the lower margins of the hardware side of the business - parts, inventory, manufacturing costs - the inevitable happened: the company rather suddenly ran out of working capital and was forced to go back to investors. And because it didn't have much "adult supervision," the company waited until things were very tight. They didn't really see it coming, and they had to pass the hat for new investment very abruptly.

Experienced investors can guess what happened at this point, too. A bunch of investors, who have not received any formal updates from the CEO, suddenly get hit with a panicked message about how the company was out of cash and needed a speedy transfusion to stave off death. Of course investors were ticked off, but it went deeper than that. The foundations of their confidence in the company were badly shaken. *They had invested primarily because they trusted the judgement and capabilities of this CEO.* They were not deep experts in the company's technology or markets, and everything they had seen by that point suggested the market was actually tougher for the company than people had hoped. *So if they were going to re-invest, it was going to come down entirely to how they felt about the CEO.*

But he had kept them in the dark while he flailed. He had not asked for help. He had not disclosed his problems and what he was doing to solve them. He had not reassured them that amidst the mistakes and setbacks there were still really good reasons to be optimistic about the business. He had done nothing to keep them engaged and "invested" in the company. So investors were naturally very reluctant to put a lot more money in. And so began a repeated cycle of underfunding that plagued and crippled the company for many years to come.

As you contemplate becoming a GP managing money for remote LPs, what lesson do you take from this? Do you expect to be making multiple capital calls over the life of the fund? If you are thinking of making a career out of this, do you expect to be raising a second fund?

If so, and you expect to keep a fairly steady pace of investing in new companies, your second fund will likely need to raise money from LPs before the results of the first fund have come in. With no results to judge you by, what will LPs fall back on? Of course, your communication and your reporting. You don't want to be like the CEO who goes out to ask for money after months and months of silence! Sure, over the long term, it is ultimately about the fund performance, but in the near and mid term, managing LPs is just like managing investors - **it's all about the reporting**.

Christopher has a lot of experience as both a fund GP and a fund LP, and many years being involved with public company investor relations and keeping Wall Street analysts happy. Let's get his perspective on key fund reporting issues.

Q

Christopher, what information does a fund manager need to gather to properly track the performance of an early stage venture fund?

LPs are going to need to see investment-by-investment data in addition to overall fund performance data. In many cases they will even expect to see data at the round-by-round level not just at the company level since different rounds in each company can have very different IRRs. To report with that level of detail, you have to have the underlying data points.

To be able to track performance of a priced equity investment on a round-by-round basis, you are going to need to gather and track the following key data points:

• Date you made the investment (it may be easier to use the date the round closed, but it is more accurate from an IRR perspective

to track from when you took the money out of the fund and committed it to the company)

• The exact amount of investment into the round, and

• Capitalization details such as the pre-money and post-money valuation so that you can accurately track the price paid per share.

To be able to track performance of a convertible debt investment on a round-by-round basis, you are going to need to gather and track the following key data points:

• Date you made the investment (since convertible note rounds tend not to have defined closing dates)

• The exact amount of investment into the round

• The cap on your conversion price

• Whether there is any discount on that conversion price

• Whether there is any interest rate being paid, and if so, what type (simple, cumulative, non-cumulative) and how frequently it is being calculated (daily monthly, quarterly, annually), and

- Whether there are any warrants or other derivatives being issued as part of the deal.

You are going to need to remember to convert your notes into stock holdings at the appropriate per share price when a qualifying round occurs and your debt converts to equity. You will also need to keep separate track of any interest earned for tax purposes, and if some note holders received warrants and others did not, you are going to have to watch out for imputed income for the delta between what you paid and what others paid. The value of the warrants is typically viewed as taxable imputed income by the IRS. The tax issues with notes can be pretty complicated, so you will want to consult an experienced tax advisor.

Finding all this data and recording it accurately can be a little bit of work, but it is as easy as it is ever going to get right after you write the check. You have all the final drafts of the

documents handy. You have the deal particulars top of mind. And you likely have contact details and telephone numbers for people to ask if you have questions right near the top of your inbox. If you let time go by, you only succeed in turning a small chore into a big pain in the neck as you struggle to collect all the relevant information and reconstruct the deal from the scattered historical pieces.

> Finding all this data and recording it accurately can be a little bit of work, but it is as easy as it is ever going to get right after you write the check.

Finding this data amidst all the deal documents is not that hard once you know where to look. With a little practice you can learn pretty quickly how to move around in the documents and find and record what you need to have in your records. If you have trouble figuring out where to find things, you can see our guides to convertible note documents and preferred stock documents in the Appendix.

A word of caution for those who might be tempted by shortcuts when gathering this data. This is a case where you really need to go back to the primary documents. You cannot pull this information out of the termsheet. Termsheets lack sufficient detail and the final deal documents often differ slightly from the termsheet, as things like the exact size of the round change or price per share change as the deal is finalized. And even if you do go back to the official deal documents, it is an extremely good practice to ask the company for a post-closing cap table. Not only is reviewing the cap table a really good way to cross-check your arithmetic on things like your ownership percentage, older cap tables tucked away can be a very handy historical record for questions down the road. This is a habit you really should get into for every round - even rounds in which you do not participate. A series of historical cap tables can be a vital tool in double-checking your payout in the event of an exit or trouble-shooting discrepancies in later rounds.

Of course, once you have collected all this data, you need somewhere to put it. You can stick it in flat files like notes or spreadsheets, but fund management tools like Seraf can be a much better solution for three reasons:

- It is designed to walk you through what you need - a place for everything and everything in its place

- It continuously leverages the data you enter so that you are running real-time performance reporting at all times.

- You generate reports at the push of a button instead of having to pull the data together and calculate performance each time.

A word of caution for those who might be tempted by shortcuts when gathering this data. This is a case where you really need to go back to the primary documents. You cannot pull this information out of the termsheet.

Q

What are the key metrics that every early stage fund manager should track to measure their fund's performance relative to other early stage venture funds? What information do I need to include when sending out a report to the fund's Limited Partners?

Reporting on fund performance is best thought of like an onion or a Russian nesting doll: from the center outward, you are addressing increasingly broad contexts:

- At the center, there is the question of how a particular investment in a particular round performed

- Then, how that company has performed

- Then, how your overall fund has performed

- Then, how that fund compares to similar VC funds of the same vintage

- And finally, how those VC vintage returns compare to broader

market averages - the returns your LPs could have achieved in other less risky more liquid investments.

Different LPs may vary in their patience, forgiveness and attention to detail, but overall, this is a very well-quantified business and there is really nowhere to hide in terms of performance and reporting.

For your day-to-day, quarter-to-quarter reporting, you are going to focus on changes to the inner circles: new rounds, new companies, updated valuations and fund performance since the last report. But the reality of the venture industry is that your micro-reporting is always happening in a macro context. This is a very well-quantified industry and you are always going to be compared to other early stage venture funds and to broader markets by various rating agencies such as major player, Cambridge Associates. And, over time, your fundraising success will be gated by how you perform in those comparisons.

To help you figure out how to construct your reporting, let's look at a menu of the potential contents of a typical quarterly or annual report. The report will be customized for each LP to reflect their specific holdings, but certain "fund overview" elements will be the same for every LP, so we have broken it down that way. This list is intended to be fairly comprehensive for educational purposes, so your final report design might not need to include every item.

This is a very well-quantified industry and you are always going to be compared to other early stage venture funds and to broader markets by various rating agencies such as major player, Cambridge Associates.

Common "Fund Overview" Elements Included in All Regular Statements and for all LPs

- Table of holdings

- Portfolio Company Updates - Section of the report with brief written updates on each company (can be at the end of the report but must include company name, website, industry, brief product description, followed by a paragraph giving an update on the company's status)

- Fund's Investment Basis and Current Valuation

- Current Total (fund holdings) Value to Paid- In Capital (TVPI)

- Change in Value over the past quarter (qtr) and year to date (ytd)

- IRR if liquidated at current valuation

- Residual Value to Paid- In Capital (RVPI)

- Total Cash Returned

- Distributed to Paid- In Capital (DPI)

- Valuation + Cash Returned

- Combined Exit Multiple

- Cumulative IRR from all Exits to date

- Changes in the portfolio holdings during quarter: New Companies/

Funds, New Rounds, Amount Invested, Amount Returned

- Portion of fund's value per company

- Transactions during quarter

- Investments and returns per each year

- Investments and returns with returns matched to original year of investment

LP Specific Measures to be Reported on a Per LP Per Statement Basis

- Capital Committed, Capital Called, Amount Outstanding

- Fees Paid

- Table of holdings reflecting LP's percentage ownership

- LP's Investment Basis and Current Valuation reflecting LP's percentage

- Change in Value over the past qtr and ytd reflecting LP's percentage

- Total Cash Returned reflecting LP's percentage

- Valuation + Cash Returned reflecting LP's percentage

- Changes in the portfolio: New Companies/Funds, New Rounds, Amount Invested qtr, Amount Returned qtr reflecting LP's percentage

Industry Comparison Benchmarks Which Will Be Applied to Your Fund Regardless and Should Be Included in Reporting

- Categorizations in terms of your fund's size, focus, region, using standard VC industry classifications

- Pooled Return of Similar Funds Compared to Public Market Equivalents on a 1-Year, 3-Year, 5-Year and longer basis

- Since Inception IRR & Multiples by Fund Vintage Year

- Since Inception IRR & Multiples Compared to Public Market Equivalents on a 1-Year, 3-Year, 5-Year and longer basis

- Since Inception IRR Based on Fund Focus, i.e. compared to

similarly focused funds and fund sizes

- Since Inception IRR Based on Fund Region, i.e. compared to funds in your region

- Since Inception IRR by Company's Initial Investment Year i.e. compared to the general returns of investments in those industries that year.

And a final note on very specific types of funds such as impact funds, university funds, or other affiliated funds: there are many additional measures that may be appropriate for special kinds of funds. Social Impact funds may want to measure the impact they are having (jobs created, additional money attracted from other investors, founder gender or ethnicity, etc.). Funds focused on geographical diversification may want to include geographical measures such as holdings by region or state. Industry sector funds may want to have special sector-specific measures relating to that industry sector. I go into more

detail on social impact investor metrics below.

> If the regular written reports are about keeping LPs informed, the other channels are about building enthusiasm, rapport and credibility and showing a little bit more of your personality and the firm's culture and mode of operating.

Q

Besides written quarterly and annual reports, in what other ways should I communicate with my Limited Partners?

If the regular written reports are about keeping LPs informed, the other channels are about building enthusiasm, rapport and credibility and showing a little bit more of your personality and the firm's culture and mode of operating. Methods of rapport-building include a variety of things - obviously the bigger funds with more resources will be able to do more - but here are a few examples:

Regardless of size, you should plan annual meetings between fund management and LPs. Most funds should consider an annual social event for LPs that also includes portfolio CEOs. Rapport can be built through events which serve a dual purpose (i.e.community-building as well as investor relations): theme oriented events and conferences, possibly with social or cocktail components afterwards, or community events or open-houses where LPs are on the guest list. Even if they don't come, it shows the LPs that the fund is active and engaged in its community.

It is also a good idea to keep track of where all your key LPs are located and try to include a meal or a coffee with them when you are traveling in or near their city. You don't want to impose too much on their time, so make sure they are keen to do it, but making the offer can go a long way in building rapport. In so doing, you will want to be careful about selectively disclosing material information to some LPs but not others. The SEC rules applicable to VCs funds are much less restrictive than those governing mutual funds and listed companies, but you would not want to have LPs question whether you are fair, even-handed and above board at all times.

Other outreach modes that are worth considering, because of their brand- and reputation-building potential, include blogs, social media feeds such as a Twitter or Instagram account, podcasts or speaking engagements. These approaches may be less direct with respect to LPs because they may be positioned as advice for entrepreneurs, or general commentary on company building or the VC industry. But, they are worth considering because they build credibility and brand awareness with both prospective entrepreneurs and prospective LPs. They also allow your LPs to tune in if they have the time or interest, but tune out and focus just on your objective reporting if their plate is very full.

Q

Social Impact investors are interested in more than just financial results. What are some of the Key Performance Indicators (KPIs) that you see tracked?

Social impact funds have a more complicated reporting challenge than traditional venture funds. Impact investing is an approach, currently enjoying growing recognition and interest, that questions whether the traditional direct philanthropy and grant-making approach is actually the best or only way to affect social good. Impact investing instead looks to leverage "fund" and "investment" paradigms with pooled assets, active managers and reinvested returns as the vehicle for change. This approach is notably different in that it seeks to use some of the financial returns to subsidize the goals of the cause in the future, which can provide significant additional leverage compared to "one and done" grant-making.

There are at least as many different kinds of impact measures as there are social causes. Ultimately, each fund GP is going to have to come up with a measurement framework that fits the social goal they are tracking and resonates enough with their potential LPs.

Obviously, impact LPs are looking for non-financial kinds of returns. Yet, they often view the financial returns as very important as well - in some cases because they are unwilling to forgo the financial gains and in other cases because they view the financial success as the key to the fund's governance and discipline, and they think it magnifies the long-term reach, might and sustainability over time. So, in addition to reporting on many or all of the traditional financial reporting metrics discussed above, the managers of social impact funds have to come up with measures of performance that allow them to account for their non-financial social impact performance as well.

There are at least as many different kinds of impact measures as there are social causes. Ultimately, each fund GP is going to have to come up with a measurement framework that fits the social goal they are tracking and resonates enough with their potential LPs. In an attempt to boil down the sea of potential social metrics, one influential paper (published by both Harvard Business Review and Stanford Social Innovation Review - "Measuring the Impact in Impact Investing") attempts to group measurement approaches into four broad categories: expected returns methods, theory of change methods, mission alignment methods and experimental methods. Here is an overview of the differences between those measures, quoted from the Stanford paper, but abbreviated for clarity:

"**Expected return methods** weigh the anticipated benefits of an investment against its costs; social return on investment (SROI), in particular, provides a framework to calculate an investment's present social value of impact compared to the value of inputs. For example, the Robin Hood Foundation's benefit-cost ratio (BCR) estimates the poverty-fighting benefits of a program compared to the costs to the foundation in order to determine which grants would yield high impact. Robin Hood computes its BCR on an ongoing basis, and during the re-investment or re-granting process it may increase investment in programs with high BCRs...

"**Theory of change methods** outline the intended process for achieving social impact, often using a logic model, a tool that maps the linkages between input, activities, output, outcomes, and ultimately impact. When estimating impact, [the team] uses a logic model to identify assumptions in an intervention's theory of change that may need further review (for example, would x output really translate into y outcome?). Logic models also help assess impact risk, the factors that could jeopardize the expected social impact of an intervention...

"**Mission alignment methods** measure the execution of strategy against the project's mission and end goals over time, using rubrics such as scorecards to monitor and manage key performance metrics on operational performance, organizational effectiveness, finances, and social value. Meaningful analysis often compares current key performance indicators to a historical baseline, to an original forecast, or to those of industry peers...

"**Experimental and quasi-experimental methods** are after-the-fact evaluations that use randomized control trials or other counterfactual approaches to determine the impact of an intervention compared to the situation if the intervention had not taken place. Where possible, [the team draws on] data from previous studies when assessing a new potential investment's impact risk. Various social impact bonds have also employed quasi-experimental and experimental methods to evaluate a program's impact, which determines the financial return on investment."

Ultimately, whatever set of impact metrics you chose should be clearly highlighted in your fundraising materials so that it is clear to LPs that financial returns are not the only, or possibly not the top, goals of your fund. And you are going to have to work extra hard to come up with a quarterly and annual reporting template which conveys a massive array of complex measures in a balanced and comprehensive way. Not a task for the faint-hearted!

If you have made it this far, you have begun to develop an appreciation for the ins and outs of the venture capital industry. This is not a job that just anyone can waltz quickly into. Even if only to raise money, let alone to be successful, an aspiring fund manager is going to need to develop a fund strategy that speaks to their skills and reach, as well as to the particular market moment. And that will include a fund design and target investment that is appropriate for the size of the fund.

Fundraising will be the next challenge an aspiring fund manager will face, and this long, grueling and inefficient process is often where many would-be fund managers get off the bus. There is tons of money out there looking for active investment managers, but there is also lots of competition and transparency, so new fund managers are going to need to bring something pretty compelling to the table if they plan to raise serious money. To be realistic, it is almost impossible to raise a fund if you do not already have some kind of track record investing in the

intended space, or an entrepreneurial track record of delivering significant start-up success.

If you do succeed in collecting a pile of money to manage, you are going to have to wade through a fairly significant process of legal and accounting to set up the fund and on-board your LPs. And you are going to have to build a fairly rigorous reporting regime if you plan to stay in the industry. Not only does reporting help you maintain the necessary level of rigor, it allows you to culture happy LPs who might consider re-investing with you in your next fund.

Once you get your fund up and running, you and your GP team are going to be close to sprinting through a fairly demanding and multidimensional job. You need the skills and contacts to fill a large funnel of excellent opportunities, the analytical abilities to sift and winnow them down into a manageable number of investable opportunities, the attention to detail to negotiate deal terms which represent a fair allocation of the myriad risks and significant upsides associated with this asset class, and finally you need the temperament, knowledge and skills to help your investments navigate the roller coaster ride that is the startup journey.

And you'll need to keep that sprinting pace up for a long time before you see any of the fruits that the VC fund model has to offer. In fact, stamina and patience won't be the only essential ingredients; you will also need to be able to live off of a very modest income while you are waiting for your fund(s) to mature. In most cases a career VC will need to begin raising their next fund just as they get their prior fund to the one-third mark. That means the successful VC manager will often be raising a fund, investing a fund, tending to one or more funds and their holdings, all while reporting to LPs on each of them. This is demanding work to be sure, but also some of the most interesting and rewarding work people with the right temperament and skill set can do. Thanks for reading and best of luck to you on your fund journey!

Appendix

At Launchpad Venture Group, we provide our members with a series of guides and templates to help improve their performance as investors. In this appendix, we include example guides and templates that we use on a regular basis.

I.   **Capitalization Table with Waterfall Analysis**: This is a collection of two spreadsheets that help you model a company's capitalization table and the resulting waterfall analysis based on a variety of exit scenarios for the company. (http://bit.ly/Series_A_Cap_Table_and_Waterfall or http://bit.ly/Series_A_and_B_Cap_Table_and_Waterfall)

II.   **Modeling Tool for an Early Stage Investment Portfolio**: This spreadsheet allows you to model potential outcomes for the overall return from an early stage investment portfolio. (http://bit.ly/Seraf_Portfolio_Modeling_Tool)

III. **Guide to Preferred Stock Deals**: This section is intended to provide a quick overview of the principal documents in a fundraising where the investors are purchasing stock. These stock transactions permanently alter the capitalization of the company by adding new stockholders, who are purchasing a brand new class of stock created for them, typically a series designated class of preferred stock with special rights and privileges they have negotiated.

IV. **Guide to Convertible Note Deals**: This section is intended to provide a quick overview and explanation of the principal documents in a fundraising where the investors are purchasing convertible debt. Unlike a stock transaction, these convertible debt deals do not alter the capitalization of the company by adding new stockholders until the debt is converted into equity.

V. **Due Diligence Report**: This template is designed to result in a short, readable due diligence report. Our goal at Launchpad is to provide our investors with a 2 to 4 page summary report that is readable and comprehensive. It covers all the main areas in diligence and provides the author(s) with a structured approach. (http://bit.ly/ Due_Diligence_Report_Template)

VI. **Due Diligence Checklist**: After reading this book, you might feel overwhelmed by all the different aspects in due diligence. The Due Diligence Checklist is designed as a quick reference guide to help steer you through the various aspects of diligence. (http://bit.ly/ Due_Diligence_Checklist)

VII. **Guidelines for Successful Board Meetings**: This a collection of well-tested guidelines that will make any early stage company board more productive. (http://bit.ly/Board_Meeting_Guidelines)

VIII. **Checklist for Planning Exits**: The startup company IPO is a much rarer creature than it used to be, so most early stage companies return maximum value to their shareholders through some form of acquisition. Planning for such an exit is an ongoing responsibility for both the CEO and the board. With that challenge in mind, we put together a guide to help with this planning exercise. (http://bit.ly/Exit_Planning_Guide)

IX. **Venture Fund Economics Modeling Tool**: This Venture Fund Economics Modeling Tool is designed to help you understand compensation for a venture fund's General Partners. (http://bit.ly/Venture_Fund_Economics)

Please note that in addition to including these guides, we also provide an online version, when applicable. If you click on the URL listed next to an item, you will be able to access an online document that can save you time in creating your own version.

I. Capitalization Tables with Waterfall Analysis

Have you ever been in a situation where you are negotiating an investment with an entrepreneur and you can't agree on the pre-money valuation? Any early stage investor who makes more than one or two investments will certainly run into this issue. It's never an easy discussion, so it helps if you are prepared ahead of time with concrete facts and figures for your recommended valuation. If you do a little homework, not only might you be surprised how little difference small changes in valuation make for founders, you will also be armed to have a very educational discussion with the entrepreneurs.

Let's play out a scenario that Christopher and I ran into recently with a company in which we were looking to invest. At a high level, here are the key facts about the company today, along with a few assumptions we will make about the future of the company.

- The company is pre-revenue and needs to raise $1.25M to get their product shipping and close their first few customer deals.

- We were willing to invest at a $3.6M pre-money valuation. The entrepreneur insisted on a $4M valuation.

- We assumed the company will need an additional $5M Series B financing to get all the way to an exit.

- We assumed the Series B round will be priced at 2X the post-money valuation of the Series A round, and both rounds will be Non-Participating Preferred.

119

- We assumed that approximately 5% of the common shares are held by employees, directors and advisors.

- We assumed an exit for the company will be somewhere in the $25M to $100M range.

	$3.6M Series A Valuation	$4M Series A Valuation
$25M Exit		
Founders	$9.3M	$9.9M
Series A Shareholders	$4.6M	$4.3M
$50M Exit		
Founders	$18.7M	$19.7M
Series A Shareholders	$9.1M	$8.7M
$100M Exit		
Founders	$37.3M	$39.5M
Series A Shareholders	$18.2M	$17.3M

So, given those facts and assumptions, what difference does our requested valuation ($3.6M) versus the entrepreneur's desired valuation ($4M) actually make to the returns of each party?

Note that our $3.6M pre-money offer is 10% less than the founder's $4M pre-money expectation. The final outcome for the entrepreneur in all of the above exit scenarios shows about a 5% to 6% difference in what they will ultimately receive upon an exit. Even though it feels to the entrepreneur that our respective valuations are miles apart, the reality is about half the difference in the end.

It is probably worth pointing out to the entrepreneur that there are two further advantages for them in keeping the pre-money reasonable:

It makes it easier to bring investors into the round so that they can finish the fund-raising quickly and get back to focusing on the operations of the company. And, it means the post-money valuation will be more reasonable, which means it will be less of a yoke around their necks (see Chapter 2) as they head into the uncertainties that lie ahead and try to grow into justifying their valuation for the next round.

So hopefully you are convinced it is worth doing some modeling. But how can you easily do this type of financial modeling to help better understand valuation and exit scenarios? You need a good Cap Table and Waterfall Analysis tool.

If you perform a Google search for the term "Cap Table", you will end up with dozens of options to choose from. These options include everything from Excel spreadsheets that build simple cap tables all the way along the spectrum to complex, high-end software products that will track everything you need for a complete cap table. But we built one we think you might prefer using.

So why did we bother creating another cap table tool when there are so many options out there? We did it for several reasons:

1. We wanted a tool that was very simple to set up. We didn't want to have to enter lots of data to model a cap table.

2. We wanted a tool that allowed us to model a variety of different exit scenarios to help understand how much each shareholder would get depending on the size of the exit.

3. We wanted a tool that was free for everyone to use with no strings attached.

We chose the familiar Google Sheets platform and created two separate documents. The first sheet allows you to create a cap table with just a single Series A round of financing for very basic modeling.

Valuations, Investments and Share Price	
	Series A
Pre-Money Valuation	$3,175,000
Total Invested in Round	$1,250,000
Post-Money Valuation	$4,425,000
Price / Share	$1.25
Liquidation Preference	1
Participating Preferred	Yes ▾

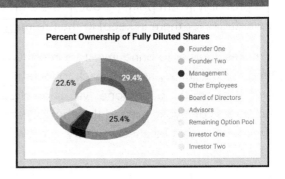

Shareholders	Common Shares	Options	Series A Preferred Shares	Series A Investment	Total Share Ownership	Percentage of Fully Diluted Shares
Shares and Options owned by the Founders of the Company						
Founder One	1,000,000		40,000	$50,000	1,040,000	29.4%
Founder Two	900,000				900,000	25.4%
Shares and Options owned by Employees, Advisors & Directors						
Management	100,000	75,000			175,000	4.9%
Other Employees		25,000			25,000	0.7%
Board of Directors		30,000	120,000	$150,000	150,000	4.2%
Advisors		10,000			10,000	0.3%
Remaining Option Pool		200,000			200,000	5.6%
Shares Acquired by Investors						
Investor One	200,000		600,000	$750,000	800,000	22.6%
Investor Two			240,000	$300,000	240,000	6.8%

Cap Table with a Series A Round of Financing

The second sheet allows you to create a cap table with both a Series A and Series B round. In both sheets, we provide a waterfall analysis so you can model exactly how much capital is returned to each shareholder and each class of stock under a variety of exit scenarios.

These sheets were designed with a fairly common capitalization structure in mind. The sheets support the following key features:

- Either one or two rounds of Series Preferred Stock
- Participating and Non-Participating Preferred Shares
- Liquidation Preferences
- Options, both Issued and Non-Issued
- Waterfall Analysis to model multiple exit scenarios

Summary Cap Table

Security Type	Outstanding Shares	Price per Share	Liquidation Preference	Percent Ownership
Common Shares	2,200,000			66%
Issued Options	140,000			4%
Series A Preferred Shares - Participating	1,000,000	$1.25	$1,250,000	30%
Total Shares Outstanding	3,340,000			

Exit Proceeds

	Price	Price	Price	Price
Purchase Price for the Company	$2,000,000	$4,175,000	$10,000,000	$20,000,000

Liquidation Preference Calculation

Series A Liquidation Preference	$1,250,000	$1,250,000	$1,250,000	$1,250,000
Remaining Proceeds	$750,000	$2,925,000	$8,750,000	$18,750,000
Proceeds per Common Share	$0.22	$0.88	$2.62	$5.61
Proceeds per Series A Share (as converted)	$0.22	$0.88	$2.62	$5.61
Total Proceeds per Series A Share	$1.47	$2.13	$3.87	$6.86

Returned Capital by Round

Common Shares	$494,012	$1,926,647	$5,763,473	$12,350,299
Options	$31,437	$122,605	$366,766	$785,928
Series A Preferred	$1,474,551	$2,125,749	$3,869,760	$6,863,772
Total Proceeds	$2,000,000	$4,175,000	$10,000,000	$20,000,000
Series A Return Multiple	1.2	1.7	3.1	5.5

Waterfall Analysis with a Series A Round of Financing

123

It's also important to note that for the sake of simplicity and usability these sheets are NOT designed to support the following items commonly found in cap tables:

- More than two rounds of Series Preferred Stock

- Convertible Notes

- Dividends

- Warrants

So, if you are looking for a complete solution that will help you manage every aspect of your company's cap table, just do a Google search and you will find plenty of great products to purchase. In the meantime, try out these free Google sheets to help you build a well structured cap table along with a waterfall analysis for exit scenario modeling.

II. Portfolio Modeling Tool

One of the biggest challenges faced by early stage investors is to assemble a portfolio of investments that in aggregate return more than 2 times the original amount invested in the total portfolio. In the language of Venture Capital, the goal of a successful early stage investor is to achieve a Distributed to Paid-In (DPI) ratio greater than 2X. In other words, for every dollar you invest in your portfolio, you want to get two dollars back over time. And, if you want to be one of the top decile early stage investors, you want to shoot for a DPI of 3X or greater.

As we discuss in Chapter 5, a successful early stage investment portfolio has a mix of strikeouts, base hits and home runs. So how is it possible for an early stage investor to build a successful portfolio compiled from companies that produce such widely different financial returns? To answer that question, we pulled together a simple modeling tool that helps you visualize how the probable returns play out and interact to produce an overall portfolio return. As usual, we built it as a Google Sheet that allows you to make a copy and model a number of scenarios for your own portfolio.

How do you go about using this modeling tool? To start, we created a sample portfolio of 15 companies for you to work from. That's enough companies to begin with for a basic portfolio modeling exercise. For each company, there are two variables that you need to set.

- First, you will need to put in an **amount that you invest in each company**. In a portfolio of 15 companies, you might have the same amount invested in each company. Or, you might decide to distribute your investments in a less even **fashion**. In the default Google Sheet, we've set up a range of investment amounts. Some companies have as little as $15,000 invested and others have as much as $50,000.

- Second, you will need to chose or "model" the **type of exit for each company** in the portfolio. Here is where you determine the multiple of capital each company will return to your portfolio. Since we are dealing with early stage companies, you will have a real mix of returns. If you want a realistic model that will be predictive of probable real-life outcomes, we recommend that you set approximately half the portfolio to total losses (i.e. no capital returned). The rest of the portfolio can be a mix of moderate successes with maybe one or two bigger wins.

Investment Portfolio

		Type of Exit	Exit Multiple
Total Amount Invested	$500,000	Loss	0
Amount of Capital Returned	$1,335,000	Breakeven	1
Distributed to Paid-In (DPI) Capital Ratio	2.67	Base Hit	4
		Home Run	10
		Grand Slam	25

Individual Investments: Exit Types and Returns

Company Name	Total Investment	Percentage of Portfolio	Type of Exit	Total Amount Returned
Investment 1	$25,000	5%	Loss	$0
Investment 2	$50,000	10%	Base Hit	$200,000
Investment 3	$25,000	5%	Loss	$0
Investment 4	$15,000	3%	Base Hit	$60,000
Investment 5	$50,000	10%	Home Run	$500,000
Investment 6	$25,000	5%	Loss	$0
Investment 7	$15,000	3%	Loss	$0
Investment 8	$50,000	10%	Breakeven	$50,000
Investment 9	$25,000	5%	Base Hit	$100,000
Investment 10	$25,000	5%	Breakeven	$25,000
Investment 11	$25,000	5%	Loss	$0
Investment 12	$50,000	10%	Base Hit	$200,000
Investment 13	$50,000	10%	Base Hit	$200,000
Investment 14	$20,000	4%	Loss	$0
Investment 15	$50,000	10%	Loss	$0
Totals	$500,000	100%		$1,335,000

There is one other variable that you can control on this sheet. In the upper right quadrant of the sheet is a section for the Exit Multiple for each type of exit. We provide values for each exit type, but you might want to model using different exit multiples. So feel free to change these numbers to fit your needs.

Once you set the two variables for each company (and make any changes to the Exit Multiples), take a look in the upper left quadrant of the Google Sheet. There are three important metrics that are calculated for you in that section.

1. **Total Amount Invested**: This is the sum of all the investments you made in the portfolio and lists the total.

2. **Amount of Capital Returned**: This is the sum of all the returned capital based on the types of exits you set for each company.

3. **Distributed to Paid-In (DPI) Capital Ratio**: This represents the multiple of capital your portfolio returns. Remember, a solid DPI is 2 and a top quartile investor will have a DPI of 3 or greater.

As we discuss above, a DPI of 2X is a good target to aim for. And 3X is even better and puts you in league with the best VCs.

One final thought to keep in mind. This tool is helpful to determine your overall multiple of returned capital. However, it does not factor in the amount of time it took for this capital to be returned. As you are building your own early stage portfolio, make sure you watch out for how long it takes to get a return on your capital. If your returns take significantly more than 10 years to appear, your resulting IRR returns will be much less than optimal. You won't earn enough for the risk you are taking and you might be better off investing in the public stock markets!

III. Guide to Preferred Stock Deals

Given the permanent capitalization changes within a preferred stock deal and the associated complexity of these transactions, there are a great number of different types of deal documents used in stock transactions. For the purposes of clarity, we've divided them into Commonly Used and Occasionally Used. Readers should also keep in mind that this chapter talks in generalities. We will describe where concepts are typically covered in a given set of deal documents. Every deal is different and a given issue may be addressed by counsel in a different way or in a different document in your deal.

Commonly Used Deal Documents in Stock Transactions

Term Sheet

Most deals start with or are accompanied by a term sheet or memorandum of understanding summarizing the terms of the deal. Unless a term sheet expressly states that some or all of its sections are legally binding, early stage investment term sheets generally are not legally binding agreements. Term sheets can be thought of as a set of notes outlining the principal elements of the deal as agreed by the negotiating parties. They serve as a basis for soliciting interest from prospective investors as well as a guide for use by counsel drafting up the definitive binding documents.

Stock Purchase Agreement

The SPA is the core document of any stock transaction. Its purpose is to document and transact the sale and issuance of the actual stock, as well as to specify key terms of the deal and allocate key risks between buyer and seller.

The main sections of an SPA typically include representations and warranties by the company and the founders as to the legal and financial status of the company and its shares, the seller's right to enter into the transaction, and other important factual matters (tightly coupled with the Disclosure Schedules discussed below). There is also a section where buyers of the stock make some representations and warranties back to the seller, and a section where the buyers impose conditions which must be met before they are obligated to buy - this section often reads like a laundry list of the other transaction documents which must be in place simultaneously. And the final section is typically a long "miscellaneous" or "other matters" section containing agreements on how the SPA will be interpreted and enforced, and documentation as to agreements on other legal matters.

Disclosure Schedule (or Schedule of Exceptions)

The disclosure schedules are technically part of the SPA and work in concert with the section on company representation and warranties. Notwithstanding that, the disclosure schedule is worth mentioning separately because (i) it is invariably prepared as a separate parallel document alongside the SPA (and is typically not finalized until the last minute) and (ii) it contains key factual data and reference information about the company which may be useful to you later.

The way disclosure schedules typically work is that the SPA says in SPA section x.x: "the company has no material contracts except as listed in section x.x of the disclosure schedule" or in SPA section y.y "the company has no shares outstanding except those listed in SPA section y.y of the disclosure schedule" or in SPA section z.z "the company is not party to any litigation other than that listed in SPA section z.z of the disclosure schedule." Often when looking for reference information about a company or tracking information for your Seraf account, you can find key bits and pieces in the disclosure schedule.

Investor Rights Agreement (also sometimes Registration Rights Agreement)

The IRA is where certain rights and privileges of the new stockholders are documented. The most common rights in an IRA are (i) the right to have your stock registered with the SEC as part of an IPO, so that they are freely tradable and liquid (typically after a lock-up period of 180 days or so) and note that these registration rights are sometimes handled in a separate Registration Rights Agreement (ii) the right to receive financial and management reports and information from the company and (iii) the right to participate (i.e. purchase stock in) future financings.

IRAs sometimes also contain agreements as to the establishment and composition of board and board committees and the right of the board/ committees to approve corporate budgets and extra-budgetary expenditures.

IRAs can spell out the stockholder's rights with respect to dividends and sometimes IRAs contain rules for calculating share price in the event of a dilutive issuance, i.e. anti-dilution protection (though this provision is more typically found in the Certificate of Incorporation) or redemption rights which are the rights to force the company to redeem your shares for cash under certain circumstances. And finally, in some IRAs you will find language about the company's obligation to pay directors expenses and indemnify directors in the event of liability in connection with board service.

Voting Agreement

The Voting Agreement is the document used to ensure that all the signing stockholders vote in concert for the good of all. Sometimes it is just the new stockholders of one class coming in with the new round who sign the voting agreement and sometimes it is all stockholders. A voting agreement typically has provisions requiring signatories to vote to create the board structure agreed upon in the term sheet. They also typically contain what is referred to as a "drag along right" or "change of control drag along" which is the right to make the minority follow (vote for) the "will of the majority," as in approving the merger, acquisition or liquidation of the company. Often voting agreements require stockholders to vote to approve the issuance of all the new common stock necessary to convert preferred shares in the event a conversion is desirable. And typically they contain a provision stating that the stockholder automatically gives a proxy to a designate of the board to vote their shares in the event that they fail to vote them as required.

Right of First Refusal & Co-Sale Agreement

The Right of First Refusal & Co-Sale Agreement (ROFR & CSA) is a clean-up agreement used to document a couple of important rights typically included in term sheets, but not appropriate for the Stock Purchase Agreement. The first of two primary things a ROFR & CSA does is to ensure that no new shareholders are brought into the company without first giving the company the option to buy the shares proposed to be sold (instead of the proposed third party buyer) on the same terms as the proposed buyer. ROFR & CSAs also typically state that in the event that the company does not want to buy the shares, that right goes secondarily to the existing shareholders.

The second primary thing a ROFR & CSA does is to ensure that no existing shareholders are able to exit their shares by selling to a third party without giving other shareholders the right to participate in that sale on the same terms and on a pro rata basis.

This may sound odd and contradictory, but think of it like both a floor and a ceiling: the effect of a ROFR & CSA is to ensure that (i) if things are going well with the company, existing shareholders, who took all the early risk, have first dibs on the company's shares and (ii) that if things are not going so great, nobody is allowed to find a buyer and get out unless everyone is allowed to participate in the partial liquidity event on a proportional basis.

The remainder of the ROFR & CSA is housekeeping to ensure that the mechanics of transfer are fair and smooth and any new shareholders are appropriately bound to the terms and conditions of the original shareholders.

Certificate of Incorporation or Certificate of Amendment (Articles of Incorporation in California)

It may seem odd to include a copy of state filing in a deal like this, but the reason this document is included in most early stage equity financings is fairly clever and sensible. Here's why: for most early stage financings, a new class of preferred stock is created, and the preferences or privileges of that class of stock is recorded in the company's Certificate or Articles of Incorporation. These key rights typically include liquidation preferences (getting paid before common stock or other classes of stock), dilution protection in the event of a down round, voting rights, election of directors, dividend rights, and rights relating to conversion into common stock.

What is sensible about that? Two things: (1) State law generally requires the affirmative vote of approval by the holders of a class of shares for a negative change to any of the rights of those shares, so preferred shareholders are going to have legal protection and the right to vote on any changes to their rights and privileges. For example, Delaware law says that the holders of a class must vote to approve any change which: "Increases or decreases the aggregate number of authorized shares of the affected class(es); or Adversely affects the powers, preferences, or special rights of the shares of such class." (2) Because company Certificates of Incorporation are public state filings, anyone considering purchasing the stock of a company has the right to inspect the special privileges given out to the shareholders of preferred stock and know that they are getting themselves into.

Legal Opinion

Investors buying stock in a company generally require counsel for the company to stake their reputation "vouching" for the legal status of the company and the validity of the transaction. Legal opinions in this context generally start with a recitation of all of the items counsel has reviewed prior to giving the opinion (deal documents, corporate records) and then go on to say, with varying degrees of wiggle room reserved, (i) that the company is validly existing and in good standing in the state in which it is formed, (ii) that the signing of the transaction documents is legal and accompanied by the necessary approvals and consents, (iii) exactly what the outstanding capitalization of the company is, (iv) that the issuance of the stock is legal under the relevant SEC exemptions, and (v) that there is no material litigation pending. Some things may be added and some of the wording may vary, but these are the basic things investors look for in a legal opinion.

Accredited Investor Questionnaire/Certification

The vast majority of early stage equity financings are done pursuant to an exemption from the registration and disclosure requirements normally imposed by the US Securities and Exchange Commission on the sale of securities to the public. The scope of the exemption is rather narrow, and among other things, it requires that shares in exempt deals be sold only to accredited investors who are presumed to be sophisticated enough to evaluate a deal without public disclosure and wealthy enough to withstand a total loss stemming from an exempt deal. The accredited investor questionnaire is the document which investors fill out and sign to certify that they are accredited investors eligible to participate in an exempt offering. This questionnaire is not always a separate document - its concepts and certification are sometimes incorporated in the Stock Purchase Agreement or other deal document instead.

Signature Pages

Technically these are not a separate document in any sense of the word - typically this term merely refers to a separate electronic or paper file containing all the signature pages of all the deal documents collected together in one single document for the convenience of a signing party. Once signed, they are attached on your behalf to the relevant documents, counter-signed by the company and returned to you as part of the final closing documents package or "closing binder." Sometimes when looking for key numerical information about your shareholdings or other tracking information for your Seraf account, you can find key bits right next to your signature in the signature pages.

Occasionally Used Deal Documents in Stock Transactions

This section covers documents which turn up from time to time. It is not a problem or concern if they are not used in a given deal; it may just mean: (i) the issues to which they relate are covered in other agreements (ii) the issues to which they relate are not present or relevant in this particular deal or (iii) the lawyers drafting the deal documents have a different drafting style.

Capitalization Table

Early stage equity financings will often, but not always, include a detailed chart or table laying out all of the ownership positions of the different stockholders of the company including common stockholders, preferred stockholders and option and warrant holders (technically these last two are security holders not stockholders.) The capitalization table may either document the various positions before the close of the new round, after the close, or preferably both in one document. Often the Capitalization Table, or at least a high level summary of it, will be included in the Disclosure Schedule (above), but sometimes it is distributed as a stand-alone document. Often when looking for key numerical information about your shareholdings or other tracking information for your Seraf account, you can find key bits in the capitalization table. Capitalization tables often prove useful down the road (for example, when trying to double-check proper payouts in an exit), so it is not a bad idea to ask for a copy of the current cap table every time you invest in a company or sign deal documents. Then just upload them to Seraf with the round and you will always have them for reference.

Board Consent

A company must have the approval of its board to be authorized to partake in an equity financing. This approval is typically recorded in board minutes of a live meeting but sometimes permission is sought and recorded in writing by means of a unanimous written consent; in those cases, a copy of that written consent is sometimes included in the deal document package.

Stockholder Consent & Waiver

Similar to the board consent, under the Certificate of Incorporation or bylaws of a company an equity financing can require shareholder approval as well as board approval, so a stockholder consent is often included as part of the deal. Sometimes it is part of one of the principal deal documents, and sometimes it is a stand-alone document. If the rights of shareholders are being changed or cut back by the terms of the new deal, an explicit waiver of the abridged rights may be included to make it abundantly clear that everyone is onboard with the deal.

Irrevocable Proxy

In a typical equity deal, voting matters are left to the individual shareholders. The assumption is that it is relatively easy for a major investor to put together a majority block in favor of a proposal the major investor would like to see passed. Or a voting agreement is used. But in some deals, nothing is left to chance and investors are asked to assign their voting rights to an investor delegate (this assignment is called giving a proxy to a proxy holder) who can then vote the rights. This is a way of ensuring that shares get voted, blocks get neatly formed and no one has to spend effort or incur delay chasing votes for desirable outcomes. These proxy assignments are generally permanent and irreversible (hence the name irrevocable) transfers of voting rights, so if you see one in a deal package, read it carefully and make sure you are comfortable that the proxy holder's interests fully align with yours.

Indemnification Agreement

Although companies generally carry Directors' and Officers' insurance to protect directors from the damages and expenses of shareholder lawsuits alleging that they did something wrong as a director, many highly skilled and sought-after directors want additional protection if they are going to be convinced to serve. What companies do in that situation is offer to, in effect, re-insure the directors by indemnifying them (agreeing to reimburse them or "hold them harmless") for any expenses or damages they incur while doing their job competently and in good faith. The way this is recorded is in an indemnification clause in one of the principal deal documents, or as a stand-alone indemnification agreement. They are long and jargon-laden documents, but what they basically say is that if the director is doing a good job and acting in good faith, and they get sued by shareholders, the company will make them whole. There are a lot of details about the precise conditions in which such reimbursement will occur and the limits on that reimbursement, but if you see one of these, the concept is pretty simple - the company will cover the directors' costs.

Secretary's Certificate

The Secretary's Certificate is essentially a small cover sheet attesting to the authenticity and accuracy of the copies of the various deal approvals and governance documents. They are typically worded as a series of paragraphs each starting out with "attached is a true and correct copy of the…" and going on to list the bylaws, the board and stockholder resolutions approving the transaction, the names and titles of the current list of officers of the company and the certificates of good standing and legal existence from the state of incorporation. And they are signed by the secretary of the corporation (who may even be the CEO in small companies.)

Compliance Certificate

The compliance certificate is a belt-and-suspenders document intended to give investors extra protection by requiring the company's CEO to personally take responsibility for the transaction. Compliance certificates typically include statements that (i) all the representations and warranties the company has made in the deal documents are true, (ii) that the company has obtained all the consents, approvals, permits and waivers it needed to obtain, (iii) the shares being issued are duly authorized, and (iv) newly revised Certificate of Incorporation has been filed and is in effect. And they conclude with a simple signature from the CEO.

Joinder Agreement

Joinder agreements are sometimes used as an easy way to make new investors a party to existing agreements - they literally join you in with the other signatories. They typically list the specific agreements and their dates and make it clear that by signing the joinder agreement, the new investor is signing, and means to be bound by all the other agreements listed.

Founder Stock Agreement (aka Vesting Agreement or Restricted Share Agreement)

Term sheets in early-stage equity deals often require that the founders' stock be subject to forfeit in the event they leave the company. This concept is sometimes inaccurately nicknamed "founder vesting" but in fact what going on is that founders are agreeing to put a layer of contractual claw-back on top of stock they already own. Given this, "restrictions lapsing" is technically more correct language than "stock vesting," but the economics are equivalent. The claw-backs amount to an agreement that they will forfeit the stock (at a typically very low price so as to not cause a cash crunch for the company) if they leave. The vesting nickname stems from the fact that these restrictions lapse as time goes by. These arrangements are usually documented in agreements variously named things like Founder Stock Agreement or Vesting Agreement or Restricted Share Agreement. Investors are typically not a party to these, but a copy is sometimes furnished to them as proof of their existence because of the importance of the issue.

Risk Factors Statement

A list of risk factors is sometimes furnished to the investors as a way of limiting various types of liability for the company in the event that things do not go as planned or shareholders become unhappy. They literally serve as a "can't say we didn't warn you" device and work by disclosing a variety of risks associated with the investment. Example risks you might see include: the stock being offered is not registered and not liquid, the terms of your deal might be renegotiated in a later financing, the company has a limited operating history and may not be successful, the company has limited operating capital and might run out of money and either fail or need to raise more money on less attractive terms, competitors may out-compete the company, customers may not like the product, the company may not get sufficient intellectual property protection, the company may not be able to attract and retain enough good talent, etc. At most you will be required to acknowledge that you got your copy.

IV. A Guide to Convertible Note Deals

Compared to preferred stock deals, there are a smaller number of types of deal documents used in convertible debt transactions. For the purposes of clarity, we've divided them into Commonly Used and Occasionally Used. Readers should also keep in mind that this section talks in generalities in terms of where legal concepts are typically covered - every deal is different and a given issue may be addressed in a different document in your deal.

Commonly Used Deal Documents in Convertible Debt Deals

Promissory Note

The Promissory Note (or Convertible Promissory Note) is the actual debt instrument in the deal. In reality it is nothing more than a fancy I.O.U. It states the names of the lender and borrower, the date of the debt, the amount of indebtedness, the interest rate, the interest rate calculation mechanism (annual, semi-annual, cumulative, non-cumulative) and the maturity date (due date). Then, usually immediately after those terms there will be some discussion of any negotiated cap on the conversion price or discount against the conversion price if the deal features a cap or discount.

The rest of the note is typically dedicated to setting out the mechanics of converting the debt repayment into stock. In this section you will find language outlining what constitutes a qualified financing - a note-holder does not want stock in a company that is underfunded (she would rather have a cash repayment), so the concept here is to say that "it needs to be part of a pretty robust financing if you are going to convert me into stock." There is also typically some language about what happens if there is no qualified financing before the maturity date. And the final few paragraphs are the usual legal housekeeping clauses about contractual interpretation and enforcement.

Special Terms: Subordination, Security Interests and Guarantees - Occasionally notes will incorporate the concept of subordination, security interests or guarantees. These features are more typical of classic bank type debt, and less common in investor convertible debt, but they are worth mentioning because they do show up occasionally.

- **Subordination** is a legal concept where a lender agrees that its right to receive repayment is subordinate to (i.e. in a lower position or in second priority to) another lender's right to repayment. For example, most banks who have lent to a company will immediately recall their loan if the company tries to borrow from investors unless investors agree their debt is subordinate to the bank's debt.

142

- **Security Interests** are legal rights allowing the lender to more easily seize collateral in the event of a default on the loan. A note that includes a security interest is called a secured note. These security interests require additional public record state filings to perfect and they are typically signaled in the title of the instrument (e.g. Convertible Secured Note) or right near the beginning of the text.

- **Guarantees** are personal undertakings by someone involved in a corporation to repay the corporation's debt if the corporation fails or defaults on the debt. Banks typically insist on personal guarantees from CEOs before lending, and they may take a security interest in the CEO's home or some other major asset as collateral. Personal guarantees are not common with straight investor debt and probably best avoided - either you believe enough in the CEO and the concept to invest and assume the risk of failure, or you don't.

Occasionally Used Deal Documents in Convertible Debt Deals

Note Purchase Agreement

A Note Purchase Agreement (sometimes called a Subscription Agreement - see below) is a contractual wrapper that makes a note financing a little bit more formal and a little bit more like a stock financing. It typically outlines the mechanics of the closing (to make sure no individual note holders get caught out as the only ones investing), it adds in some representations and warranties on the part of the company around validity and authorization, it add some note holders reps and warranties around eligibility as an accredited investor, and in some rare cases, it may serve to cover some of the key provisions you might expect to see in a Note Holders Agreement or a Voting Agreement (both discussed below.)

143

Subscription Agreement

A note Subscription Agreement is very similar to a Note Purchase Agreement (above) - mostly it is just a naming convention. Occasionally, however, you will see subscription agreements used to take some of the more complex terms of a note out of the note itself and into a separate subscription contract such that the note and the subscription agreement work as two halves of one convertible debt deal. The effect of doing it this way is the same, it just allows for a more simple note and a more thorough treatment of conversion mechanics in a more traditional contract format.

Note Holders Agreements and Voting Agreements

Sometimes the holders of a note will wisely insist on things like board seats, information rights, covenants against issuing stock or other debt and/or other terms more typically associated with stock deals. When this happens, these contractual agreements between the company and the noteholders are usually written up in a separate agreement given a title like Note Holders' Agreement or Voting Agreement.

Subordination Agreement

Sometimes subordination of debt (see above) is done by means of a stand-alone agreement. This most often occurs when new debt is added after the debt to be subordinated is already in place - for example when there is an outstanding convertible debt round and a revolving line of credit from a bank is added, and the parties enter into a new agreement to make it clear that the old debt is subordinate to the new debt.

Warrant to Purchase Stock

One of the complaints about convertible notes in the early stage context is that they amount to equity risk for debt returns. This results in pricing incentives that lead to a misalignment of interests between company management and the investors. People try to address this with the terms of the note - for example caps on the conversion price and discounts on the conversion price. But these mechanisms do not fully align the interests of the founders and the note holders, so in an effort to better address that, sometimes warrants to purchase shares are given in lieu of or in addition to caps and discounts. It obviously makes the note perform economically more like equity since warrants literally are securities derived from equity, but warrants do introduce a bit of complexity into what is supposed to be a simple transaction.

V. Due Diligence Report

This template is designed to result in a short, readable due diligence report. Our goal at Launchpad is to provide our investors with a 2 to 4 page summary report that is readable and comprehensive. It covers all the main areas in diligence and provides the author(s) with a structured approach.

Company: {Company Name}

CEO: {CEO Name}

Report Date: {Date}

Company Description:

{insert 1-2 paragraph summary description of company here}

Due Diligence Assessment:

{This section is the heart of the due diligence report. For each topic, we provide you with example questions that make for appropriate areas to discuss in the remarks column. This report template is deliberately designed as a table to force the authors to be concise. It's important to be succinct in your diligence findings summary. Otherwise, you will end up with a long report that investors won't read through, thus defeating the purpose of the report. If you have important detail or documents that you feel must be included in your findings, you can make them into appendices and refer to them in the report, but can be a slippery slope toward an excessively long package. A better approach is to keep primary research materials and memos in a cloud folder you can make available to the minority of investors who want more detail.}

Topic	Rating	Remarks
Investment Thesis		
What Needs To Be Believed (WNTBB)		
Failure Risk		
Leadership Assessment		
Technology, IP and Product Roadmap		
Customer Need and Go-To-Market Plan		
Uniqueness and Competition		
Market Size and Market Opportunity		
Financial Projections and Funding Strategy		
Exit Strategy		
Deal Terms and Payoff		

Note: See page 150 for the Rating Key and pages 151-155 for details on what remarks to supply in each of these sections.

Individual Assessments:

{This section of the report is designed to allow each member of the due diligence team to provide some short feedback on their personal opinion of the investment opportunity. You shouldn't expect everyone's assessment to be positive. In fact, it's important to have at least one or two dissenting opinions to add balance to the report. And, make sure to ask for succinct summary comments. It is especially helpful if each commenter ends their comments with a note about whether they plan to invest and why/why not.}

Team Member	Rating	Summary Remarks
{Name 1}		
{Name 2}		
{Name 3}		

Key
(++) = Very Positive (+) = Positive (0) = Neutral
(–) = Negative but issues can be overcome
(/)Very Negative, issues cannot be overcome

Investment Thesis: This section is where you explain the overall logic of the investment and characterize how it is that investors will make money. Questions you may want to cover here include:

- Is this a billion dollar IPO opportunity or is it more likely to be acquired for under $50M? Or something in between?

- Are there limited number of risks that can be mitigated or is this a moonshot deal with big risk and potentially big reward?

- Will it take 10 years to complete the product and get FDA approval, or could this company be acquired in the first couple of years by a big competitor?

What Needs to Be Believed (WNTBB): This section is where you boil down all of the key risks that need to be assumed in order to invest (see companion eBook for more detail). If an investor cannot make peace with or cannot believe an item on this list can be overcome, she should not invest. Example WNTBBs might include:

- That this market can be disrupted.

- That enough customers will find this essential at this price point.

- That the company will be successful in transitioning from current niche to mainstream.

- That the company can build out a successful go to market plan and demonstrate traction on this round size.

- That this management team can scale to pull this off.

- That the company can achieve market share before the large competitors crowd them out.

Failure Risk: This section is where you talk about the main weaknesses in the plan and the degree to which they are mitigated. If this company fails is it likely for lack of capitalization, inability to make the technology work, competition?

Leadership Assessment: This section is where you discuss your assessment of the management team. Questions you may want to cover here include:

- Does the CEO possess the experience and leadership abilities to succeed?
- Do they have skills for where they are going, as opposed to where they have been?
- Do the CEO and team have a proven track record?
- Does the team possess the appropriate balance of experience and skill sets?
- Are the board members and advisors suitable and committed?
- What key hires are needed to address gaps?

Technology, IP and Product Roadmap: This section is where you discuss your assessment of the technology and technology risk as well as the IP situation. Questions you may want to cover here include:

- Is the technical team qualified and experienced?
- How strong are the technology and IP positions?
- Is there a product roadmap and is it achievable?
- What are the remaining risks related to technology, IP and product roadmap?
- Are their superior technologies on the near term horizon?

Customer Need and Go-To-Market Plan: This section is where you discuss your assessment of the plan to take the product to market. Questions you may want to cover here include:

- Is the GTM plan sufficiently detailed?

- Are the assumptions, including required level of sales spend and time lines reasonable?

- Is the sales pipeline adequate, and are key metrics for adoption rate, conversion rates, etc. conservative?

- Do customers confirm the need and likely adoption rates?

- Beyond verifying some demand, do we understand the customers buying priorities? Is this Oxygen, Aspirin or Jewelry?

- What are the major risks in marketing awareness, customer adoption rates and sales cycle?

Uniqueness and Competition: This section is where you discuss your assessment of the overall competitiveness and defensibility of the offering. Questions you may want to cover here include:

- Is the company well positioned with respect to current and likely future competitors?

- Is the founding team well-informed about their market and industry? Do they have a good competitive sense, or are they unaware of key issues?

- What are the major risks in marketing awareness, customer adoption rates and sales cycle?

Market Size and Market Opportunity: This section is where you discuss your assessment of the actual addressable market. Questions you may want to cover here include:

- Are the top-down and bottoms-up market estimates consistent and attractive?

- Are the market share projections reasonable?

- What are the remaining risks in market development?

Financial Projections and Funding Strategy: This section is where you discuss your assessment of the financial plan and capital raising strategy. Questions you may want to cover here include:

- Does the balance sheet make sense, and are there any showstopper issues?

- Are the financial projections reasonable and conservative in light of past performance?

- What are the implications of variances in key assumptions?

- Is the future financing risk manageable?

- What are remaining financial risks?

- Are the assumptions about scaling expense (e.g. G&A, etc.) reasonable, or is the model unrealistic?

Exit Strategy: This section is where you discuss your assessment of the likely exit opportunities. Questions you may want to cover here include:

- Is there alignment with the CEO and team on exit goals?

- Is the exit strategy reasonable?

- Is the assumed timeline reasonable?

- What exit multiples can be predicted under representative scenarios?

- Does the CEO know people in the industry? Is he/she a networker who will make the relationships and do the thought-leadership necessary to get a buyer interested?

Deal Terms and Payoff: This section is where you summarize the relationship between the deal terms in the termsheet and the expected investor return. Questions you may want to cover here include:

- Is this a low valuation, high risk deal, or a high valuation, low risk deal?

- Does the termsheet include specific terms intended to protect this round of investors?

- Can you show the desired return multiple based on exit multiples for comparable companies?

VI. Due Diligence Checklist

This checklist is designed to be appropriate for early stage investments. The "Information Request" and "Tasks" columns list those items and tasks, respectively, that are generally required, at a minimum, to complete diligence. The "Key Questions" column is representative of typical questions the diligence effort should address. The information request, tasks, and key questions should all be reviewed and revised, as needed, for the particular situation. The "Summary Points" column may be used by the team to summarize the answers to key questions in preparation for drafting the diligence report. Thank you to Launchpad member Gail Greenwald for her help developing this checklist.

Leadership Assessment

Information Request	Tasks	Key Questions
Resumes for key leadership team members	Review resumes	Does the CEO possess the experience and leadership abilities to succeed?
Professional references for key team members	Interview references (see interview guidelines)	Do they have skills for where they are going, as opposed to where they have been?
Resumes and contact info for board members and advisors	Gather additional information from network as available (asking around, checking LinkedIn - anything to find blind reference checks)	Do the CEO and team have a proven track record?
	Assign team member(s) to spend time with CEO	Does the team possess the appropriate balance of experience and skill sets?
	Assess CEO and team for leadership, integrity, track record, required competencies	Are the board members and advisors suitable and committed?
	Assess suitability and commitment of board members and advisors	What key hires are needed to address gaps?

Technology, IP and Product Roadmap

Information Request	Tasks	Key Questions
Descriptions of technology and product	Review information and meet with technical team	Is the technical team qualified and experienced?
Relevant technical publications	Assess critical technologies, tool choices, software architecture choices, scalability of solution	How strong are the technology and IP positions?
Patents and patent applications	Assess IP defensibility	Is the product roadmap achievable?
Related IP info (defense: Freedom to Operate (FTO)?, offense: enforceability?)	Conduct additional secondary research as needed	What are the remaining risks related to technology, IP and product roadmap?
Product roadmap with key milestones	Conduct additional expert interviews if needed	Are their superior technologies on the near term horizon?
Competing technologies and commercialization status	Assess remaining technical risk, IP defensibility, competitive technical position	

Regulatory Strategy

Information Request	Tasks	Key Questions
Regulatory strategy, if relevant	Review regulatory strategy	Is the regulatory strategy well thought through and feasible?
Status of dialogue with regulatory authorities and/or consultants, copies of relevant communications	Interview regulatory experts	Are the company's financial resources sufficient to implement the regulatory plan?
	Assess comparable regulatory pathways for other products as appropriate	Are assumptions about partners/acquirers' roles in the regulatory plan reasonable?
	Assess regulatory climate	What are the remaining regulatory risks?

Customer Need and Go-to-Market Plan

Information Request	Tasks	Key Questions
Go-to-market plan with key milestones and granular detail on sales approach	Review information and meet with marketing and sales team	Is the GTM plan reasonable?
Partner identification and relationship status	Interview customers, partners, prospects as appropriate	Is the sales pipeline adequate, and are key metrics for adoption rate, conversion rates, etc. conservative?
Sales pipeline by stage, factored to be truly realistic and achievable	Gather information on industry comparisons as appropriate	Do customers confirm the need and likely adoption rates?
Any current marketing, joint venture, distribution agreements	Collaborate with financial team to assess revenue and pricing model	Beyond verifying some demand, do we understand the customers buying priorities? Is this Oxygen, Aspirin or Jewelry?
Customer, prospect, and partner references (see guidelines for interviewing customers)		What are the major risks in marketing awareness, customer adoption rates and sales cycle?

Uniqueness and Competition

Information Request	Tasks	Key Questions
List of current and prospective competitors	Gather additional competitive intelligence as needed	Is the company well positioned with respect to current and likely future competitors?
Competitive analysis including market share, relative strengths and weaknesses	Assess competitive environment, competitor positions, barriers to entry	Is the founding team well-informed about their market and industry? Do they have a good competitive sense, or are they unaware of key issues?
		What are the major risks in marketing awareness, customer adoption rates and sales cycle?

VII. Guidelines for Successful Board Meetings

Running a successful board meeting requires planning and discipline, which in turn requires some experience and some guidelines. Without this preparation, you will waste precious time focusing on the wrong things. To help you orchestrate great board meetings, we pulled together a collection of well-tested guidelines that will make any early stage company board more productive. Key areas include:

- Agenda items you should cover in a company's **first board meeting**

- Typical **board calendar structure** for early stage companies

- A **high level agenda** for regular board meetings

- An **overview of the package of materials** that are sent out in advance of a board meeting

First Board Meeting Agenda

For many startup companies, you will join a board that has limited structure to both the meetings and other key governance issues. Make sure that best practices for boards are put in place early on. We recommend that the initial board meeting use the following agenda.

- Appoint Secretary (usually company lawyer), Assistant Secretary (someone to sign documents) and Secretary pro tem (writes minutes)
- Discuss appointing a Chair or Lead Director (best practice) or none (absence can lead to dysfunction over time)
- Discuss use of a company lawyer at board meetings (it can be very valuable and most lawyers will attend board meetings for free or at a very significant discount)
- Adopt stock option plan and new bylaws
- Appoint audit and compensation committees (all independent directors)
- Establish board meeting calendar for the next 6 to 12 months
- Establish standard agenda for first few meetings
- Authorize purchase of D&O Insurance
- Approve budget for first round of financing and/or year

Creating a Board Calendar

Setting an appropriate level of board meetings is not that complicated. Young companies need a bit more regular oversight than more mature companies. That said, you don't want to have the company CEO spending too much of her time prepping for board meetings and not focusing on moving the company forward. A structure we use with many of our portfolio companies is based on the following 8 meetings a year tempo.

- Full board meeting once a quarter where everyone attends in person. These meetings tend to last 3 to 4 hours.

- Phone call status meetings halfway between the quarterly meetings. These meetings tend to last 1 to 2 hours. Please note that these call in meetings are more productive if done with video conferencing. Board members tend to stay more focused when they know you can see their face!

Another best practice to help build board cohesiveness is to hold a dinner the night before the board meeting. This dinner shouldn't focus on topics related to the company. Instead, it's an opportunity for board members to get to know each other and help build the bonds needed to get the company through good times and bad.

Regular Board Meeting Agenda

Use a standard format for each of your regular board meetings – Most early stage companies will want to use the following format for their board meeting structure:

1) **Introduction**: This part of the meeting should take 30 minutes or less.

- Handle housekeeping issues such as approving minutes, option grants, etc.
- Review of the management dashboard.

2) **Strategic Discussion**: This is the core of the meeting and will take up the majority of the meeting time.

- This is where the board "earns its keep" in terms of adding business value. Helping the company address key strategic issues in areas such as product, market, team, competition and funding are what an early stage board is supposed to do.

3) **Function Review:** This is more of a report and a minority of meeting time is allocated to it.

- Invite the management team to provide an update on each department (or bring in one department per meeting for a deeper dive)
- Key department discussions include: R&D, Sales, Marketing and Finance
- Provide board interaction with the management team and give them a sense of how the board thinks and how they are held accountable by the board.

Executive Session: This special session typically occurs after the end of the main meeting, and refers to a session where the executives (including the CEO) are out of the room. It is a good practice to hold an Executive Session even if there is nothing special to discuss, because it can be very unsettling to a CEO to have one called when they are not the norm.

Gives independent board members a chance to discuss the whole management team in confidence.

Board Chair or lead director will typically be instructed to circle back to the CEO on the executive session, and there should be consensus or even explicit instructions on what to say if the topic is sensitive – many misunderstandings are born from inaccurately summarized executive sessions.

This is a good time to discuss key topics that the independent board members would like to have the CEO cover at the next board meeting.

Overview of a Board Reporting Package

There are several items that most board packs have in common. You should typically expect to find four different sets of documents:

1. Meeting Agenda,

2. Minutes from prior board meetings,

3. Financials, and

4. Slide deck with key strategic discussion topics and company status update.

Directors should read these materials in advance of the board meeting and come prepared with any clarifying questions and comments.

- Meeting Agenda – This document should be one page long, and should not make any reference to the length of discussions.

- Board Minutes – This document should be a very short and concise summary of the last board meeting and contain the list of meeting attendees and any votes acted on by the board.

- Financials – This set of spreadsheets should include the company's Profit & Loss Statement, Balance Sheet and Cash Flow Statement. It is also useful to have current vs. plan comparisons. It should include a forecast at least for the remainder of the year.

- Key Discussion / Company Status – In most cases this will be a PowerPoint deck with 15 to 30 slides. The slide deck should include: 1) repeat of meeting agenda, 2) board actions, 3) management dashboard, 4) key strategic issues for discussion, and 5) a brief status update on/from each department.

VIII. Exit Planning for CEOs and the Board of Directors

As a director on an early stage company board, how do you deliver on your main responsibility as a board member - maximizing shareholder value? And, what do you do to make sure the CEO is doing her job in increasing the value of your investment in the company? And what good is the increase in value if it is not accompanied by sufficient liquidity to realize it? Those are very important questions that very few early stage company boards take the time and effort to ask early on when it is still possible to have the biggest impact.

The startup company IPO is a much rarer creature than it used to be, so most early stage companies return maximum value to their shareholders through some form of acquisition. Planning for such an exit is an ongoing responsibility for both the CEO and the board. With that challenge in mind, we put together a guide to help with this planning exercise. CEOs should use this guide as an approach or checklist to help stay on top of who their potential acquirers are and what the company's relationship is with each acquirer. And, furthermore, CEOs should use this guide as a way to update the board on at least an annual basis.

What topics are covered in the exit planning guide for early stage companies?

For each potential acquiring company, the guide asks the following questions:

- **Status**: This really goes to awareness. What is the status of any discussions? What do they know about our company? Who are the key people we met with? Describe the key relationships we have within this acquirer? Do we need to develop additional relationships?

- **Need**: Why would the acquirer want to buy our company? Are we a "must have" or a "nice to have"?

- **Value**: What do they value us for and what kind of valuation rubric might they use? Are they buying us for our people, our technology, our product or our business? What might our company be worth to the acquirer? How will they determine the value - as a multiple of revenue or EBITDA; using a buy vs build vs partner analysis, or for some strategic reason like keeping us out of the hands of a competitor?

- **Milestones**: What milestones will we need to achieve before the acquirer will be interested?

- **Current Opportunities**: What opportunities do we have to work with the acquirer before an acquisition is made? What actions are we taking on these opportunities?

- **Appetite for Acquisition**: What acquisitions has this company made in the past few years? What price have they paid for these acquisitions?

By answering these questions with some level of detail, you will get a much better sense for what your company needs to accomplish before it's well positioned for an acquisition. Since putting all your eggs in one basket is not a great strategy, you will want to have a list of at least 5 acquiring companies and preferably more in the range of 10 to 15.

What are some of the questions a potential acquirer will ask an early stage company?

Once you reach the point where there is serious interest in acquiring your company, you will need to be prepared to answer some challenging questions. Some of these questions are specific to your company's growth plans, and we expect the CEO and board have been focused on answering these questions for quite some time.

- What are the key metrics you track to understand how your business is growing? How have those metrics been trending over the past year?

- What do you believe is the total addressable market for your business?

- Where do you see the greatest opportunities for growth in your business? What are you doing today to go after those opportunities?

- What companies do you see as your biggest competitors and what do you think differentiates your products from their products?

- How close to your annual plan have you been over the past 8 quarters? How confident are you in your projects for the upcoming 4 quarters?

Other questions will be specific to your willingness to be acquired. The buyer will want to understand your motivations and fit with their company. So be prepared with great answers to the following questions:

- What are your reasons for selling the company?

- What do you see as the most important synergies between our company and yours?

- After we complete the acquisition, what role will the CEO and her management team play in our company?

These two sets of questions are by no means complete. But, they are a starting point that will help you think about what questions are important for a potential buyer of your company. Start with these questions, add some of your own, and make sure the CEO can answer them all in a credible fashion.

Exit Planning Guide for Early Stage Companies - Part 1

Company	Status	Need	Value
Name of potential acquiring company	What do they know about our company? Who are the key people we met with? Describe the key relationships we have within this acquirer. Do we need to develop additional relationships?	Why would the acquirer want to buy our company? Are we a "must have" or a "nice to have"?	Are they buying us for our people, our technology, our product or our business? What might our company be worth to the acquirer? How will they determine the value?

Exit Planning Guide for Early Stage Companies - Part 2

Company	Milestones	Current Opportunities	Appetite for Acquisitions
Name of potential acquiring company	What milestones will we need to achieve before the acquirer will be interested?	What opportunities do we have to work with the acquirer before an acquisition is made? What actions are we taking on these opportunities?	What acquisitions has this company made in the past few years? What price have they paid for these acquisitions?

IX. Venture Fund Economics Modeling Tool

This Venture Fund Economics Modeling Tool is designed to help you understand compensation for a venture fund's General Partners. The overall structure of the worksheet is quite simple.

There are two main areas where you supply information into this worksheet: 1) Fund Size, Fees and Results and 2) Payments to Partners and Fund Operations. Based on your inputs, Total Compensation for the different partners is calculated. Please note that you can add data into any cell that is filled in yellow. All grey cells should not be changed as they contain formulas.

Fund Size, Fees and Results

Fund Size	$50,000,000	Total Capital Invested	$42,500,000
Management Fee	2%	Management Fee Payout	$7,500,000
Carry	20%	Carry Payout	$15,000,000
Distributed to Paid-In (DPI) Capital Ratio	2.50	Multiple on Capital Invested	2.94

Payments to Partners and Fund Operations

	Managment Fee Allocation	Management Fee	Carry Percentage Allocation	Carry	Total Compensation
General Partner 1	20%	$1,500,000	45%	$6,750,000	$8,250,000
General Partner 2	20%	$1,500,000	45%	$6,750,000	$8,250,000
Venture Partner	10%	$750,000	8%	$1,200,000	$1,950,000
Fund Operations Team & Expenses	50%	$3,750,000	2%	$300,000	$4,050,000
Totals	100%	$7,500,000	100%	$15,000,000	$22,500,000

Fund Size, Fees and Results: There are 4 variables to supply in this section.

1. First, you need to enter the **Fund Size**. This represents the total amount of capital committed to the fund by the Limited Partners and the General Partners.

2. Next, the **Management Fee** is the annual fee paid out to run the fund. This fee is paid as a percentage of the total fund size. In this spreadsheet, the full management fee is paid out in the first 5 years. For the second 5 years of the fund, 1/2 of the management fee is paid out. So, for example, for a $50M fund with a 2% management fee, a management fee of $1M will be paid in each of the first five years. During the next 5 year period, $500K will be paid.

3. Next, **Carry** is the percentage of the fund's profits that are paid out to the General Partners.

4. And finally, the **Distributed to Paid-In (DPI) Capital Ratio** is the total amount of capital returned to investors divided by the total amount of capital invested in the fund.

Payments to Partners and Fund Operations: There are two variables you need to provide in this section.

1. The first is the **Management Fee Allocation**. For the General Partners, Venture Partners and Fund Operations, you should allocate a percentage of the annual management fee. Think of this allocation as you would allocate expenses in a business.

2. The **Carry Percentage Allocation** is where most of the compensation for a venture fund will come from for the General Partners. In most cases a fund will allocate the majority of the payout to the GPs and reserve a smaller amount for any venture partners and some of the fund's staff.

Once you've entered these variables you will be able to accurately assess compensation.

This book is brought to you by the founders of **Seraf**. Seraf is a web-based portfolio management tool for investors in early stage companies. Seraf's intuitive dashboard gives angel investors the power to organize all of their angel activities in one online workspace. With Seraf, investors can see the combined value of their holdings, monitor company progress, analyze key performance metrics, track tax issues, store investment documents in a cloud-based digital locker, and more. Seraf's easy interface enables investors to track their early stage portfolios as efficiently as they track their public investments. To learn more, visit **Seraf-Investor.com**.

Hambleton Lord is Co-Founder of Seraf and the Chairman of Launchpad Venture Group, an angel investment group focused on seed and early-stage investments in technology-oriented companies. Ham has built a personal portfolio of more than 60 early stage investments and is a board member, advisor and mentor to numerous start-ups.

Seraf Co-Founder **Christopher Mirabile** is the Chair Emeritus of the Angel Capital Association and also Managing Director of Launchpad Venture Group. He has personally invested in over 75 start-up companies and is a limited partner in four specialized angel funds. Christopher is a frequent panelist and speaker on entrepreneurship and angel-related topics and serves as an adjunct lecturer in Entrepreneurship in the MBA program at Babson. Due to their combination of roles as investors, advisors and angel group leaders, Ham and Christopher were named among Xconomy's "Top Angel Investors in New England."

Made in the USA
Middletown, DE
01 August 2023

36111598R00106